DIVINE EMOLE

A GUIDE TO BUILDING INTENTIONALLY

First Published In Nigeria:
Copyright © 2012
Divine Imole
Independently published

ISBN: 9789789952083

Cover designed by:
Onyekachi Ezenwanili
(AKA Dr. Poe of Poe International)

For permission requests write to the author at
divineemole@gmail.com

DEDICATION

To my darling wife, Bliss who is my support system, a personal source of encouragement and inspiration, and a cause for my passionate commitment to building lasting legacies.

To my boys, Charisma and Doxazo, whose time and convenience was continually disrupted during the development of this work.

To every leader, entrepreneur and builder who is building legacies in these days where people literally run away from processes that make the great.

To all the individuals whom I have had the privilege and opportunity to inspire to strive to be all they were born to be.

To the millions of great men and women who presently occupy the wombs of their mothers, children destined to change the world and become the builders of great institutions and legacies.

Contents

DEDICATION iii

ACKNOWLEDGMENTS vi

INTRODUCTION **9**

Created a Creator 9

CHAPTER ONE **12**

Build That Thing 12

CHAPTER TWO **30**

The Planning Factor 30

CHAPTER THREE **43**

The place of intellect and psychological power 43

CHAPTER FOUR **52**

The Process Factor 52

CHAPTER FIVE **64**

How God builds 64

CHAPTER SIX **81**

B---Bravery 81

CHAPTER SEVEN **88**

U—Understanding 88

CHAPTER EIGHT **95**

I—Impact 95

CHAPTER NINE **112**

L-everage 112

L-eadership 112

CHAPTER TEN 122

D-Determination 122

ACKNOWLEDGMENTS

This work is a product of the intelligent synergy of many great minds. I am forever grateful to the inspiration and wisdom of the many great men and women who, through their commitment and passion, have left a legacy to motivate me and my generation by the things they built.

I am grateful to the great men and minds that God used to build me and still building me along my path of life and destiny; First of all of them are Elder and Mrs Emole A. Kalu (my parents), Dr and Mrs Don Odunze Snr. (picked me up immediately after high school and exposed me to the wits of building a great life, Dr and Mrs Edwin Biayeibo took the crude and raw young man, trained, mentored and made sure that focus was established, The Metropolitan Paul Adefarasin for being a great father and giving me the platform to contribute to the building of men and legacies.

For the development and production of this book, I feel a deep sense of gratitude to: My wonderful wife, Bliss, and our children for their contribution, patience, understanding, and support during my many commitments and involvements outside the home. You make it easy for me to fulfill God's will. The production team of this book are simply exceptional. The great minds of Miracle, Chukwuamaka, Kachi (Dr. POE), Somadina, Dr. Blessing made this work the class it is.

I am also grateful for the members and Leadership at House On the Rock, Umuahia. Their faithful prayers, patience, and loyalty inspire me and allow me to build and fulfill my purpose and potential.

And finally, to the Builder of all things, the Source and

Supplier of all potential, the Omnipotent One, the Father and Lord of all creation; His Son, my elder Brother, Jesus Christ; and my personal Counselor, the Holy Spirit. Thank you Lord for the privilege of serving you.

Rev. Dr. Edwin Biayeibo BL, MSBM, MBA, LLB, Ph.D
Regional Director (South East Nigeria), House On The Rock.
Chief facilitator and Visionary Officer (CFVO) of D.I.P Consulting Ltd

---

This is a truly insightful and thought-provoking book that simply captures the essence of what it is to be genuinely focused, intentional, and effective in creating a successful and purposeful life.

With artful clarity and relatable examples, Divine Emole (PD) masterfully synthesized and spelled out the principles and techniques that can allow for the readers to better recognize, understand, and put into action their own natural abilities to grow exponentially in any and all areas of their lives.

BUILD is a conversation-starter and a must-read manual for anyone who wants to be fully present in building and growing better in a smarter way.

Dr. Blessing A. Okoro Rellias, PhD, LMFT, CAP, CCTP
Founder & CEO, IntegraLife Health & Wellness Institute, California, USA

BUILD is a must read for anybody who is intentional about success, the detailed expository nature of this book makes it easy to assimilate and understand.

The smooth blend between faith and practicality makes BUILD relevant to people of all faith, tribe, vocation and interest.

This book has the capacity to transform any individual to a solid success; I will advise that anybody who doesn't want to succeed should avoid this book because this book will make it impossible to fail again in life.

This book will give you the tools to build intentionally and successfully in any area of your life.

I recommend BUILD as a proven manual for success.

Dr. Emerie Agunwah
President, Marina Group

So much is required to build, and much more to build anything that is timeless, impactful and meaningful. I have read so many materials on Building, Purpose, Planning, Process, Leadership, Impact etc, but this is one book that assembles these and more principles and concepts into a concise practical guide to living a meaningful and fulfilling life on earth, as originally designed by God. Backed by the Scriptures and the writer's experiences, this book could easily be considered a life compass.

Engr. Okechukwu Eze
ED, Business Services & Operations, TENECE GROUP.

Introduction

"

For every house is builded by some man but he that built all things is God.
Hebrews 3:4

Created a Creator

There are four kinds of people that live on the face of the earth. There are people that watch things happen, these are the onlookers otherwise known as spectators. There are people that document the things that happen, these ones are usually the critics and analysts, and they end up chronicling the achievements of others. There are those that make things happen, these ones are the highflyers, the eager beavers or the ones we refer to popularly today as go-getters. Finally, we have those that wonder what happened; these ones have a comfortable apartment in oblivion while they still live. I realized that in life, bodies are at risk of being moved by things should they remain at rest for too long. If you don't drive yourself, things will drive you. There is no such thing as a stagnant place in life, there is nothing like stagnant water, what we call stagnant water is deep floating water. There's nothing like stagnation in life.

One of my mentors told me that the easiest way to backslide is to stay at a place when others are making progress. You'll think you are still standing at a place while life has left you behind. By the time you become aware of your life and where you are, you'll find out that you are far behind.

If you don't cultivate your farm, things will still grow on it, they are called weeds. If you leave water for too long in a bowl and come back after some time you will realize that some things have started growing in the bowl; this is because spaces are meant to be occupied. God created us to build, not just waste spaces and time. We are created to improve on the things we've been given.

Permit me to tell you that God is no longer building anything? God has finished building. If there are things to be built, they are in our hands. Every day there are new discoveries. Why are they called discoveries? They are called that because they were there but were not seen before the time of their discovery. The next invention is just around the corner waiting for the eye, keen enough to find it out.

The raw material that God uses to build is his word. If his word is settled that means he has finished creation, man's hand is the court wherein lies the ball of continuing creation. God is looking at man now to start discovering and building in the physical what He has built in the spiritual. Everything he has given, he left in its raw state, and the onus now rests on us to either invent or innovate. If you want cloth God will not give you cloth. He has given us a tree called cotton; he has given us animal hide. So, man looks at it and builds according to the specification of his necessity. You want things to turn a turbine, I have given you crude oil, says the Lord. Get it out, science calls it fractional distillation, the more you heat it, it separates, something new comes out; Paraffin oil, PMS, diesel etc. Even the last thing that is called waste in crude oil is not waste, it's medicinal.

Look at this phrase, "He that built". Do you see that he is done building? Therefore, from what he has built, build your own. He will not give you cement; he will give you a combination of Calcium, Carbon and Carbonate, Trioxocarbonate (IV). It will be under the ground as limestone, but you get cement out of it. While you are getting cement, the residue you can use for chalk. Every house has its builder. The truth is that if you are not building, you'll be someone else's building material.

Every man is created to be a producer. Every man is created to produce something. I realized that the greatest resource you need is not even money, it's YOU! You are your foremost and most essential resource. Every now and then, you get to find fresh graduates talking about business, get close and ask them why they've not started the business, they'll tell you: "no capital". Such persons forget that they are the capital. Can your goodwill raise you funds? Can your resourcefulness raise your capital? Can somebody look at you and say: "I know this thing will not fail because you're in it, let me invest in it". Can you go to somebody and say: "Please give me this" and the person grants it simply because you asked?

I have seen people build multimillion-dollar businesses from no money. They just received goods on trust from people who told them to sell, bring back all the proceeds of their sales except the profit and come back the next day for another on account of a successful transaction. I know one such person who did that for one year, after which he was able to raise enough cash to order for goods. What started the business was not money, it was goodwill; it was trust. If I gave you goods worth #500, 000, can I count on you to bring back returns of #500, 000 when you are done? I can testify for two people I know who have built businesses this way. One looked at our church and said daddy you have moved to a tent and you didn't tell me. He asked me what was remaining and I told him what we needed, immediately he asked for our account details, and sent in some money, with which we were able to procure about two doors. When he started the business, he started small. He sells food, you'd think it's a big restaurant, it's not for now but the young man is doing well. If you meet him, you'll be shocked at his age. He started with a "Bukka" and one table; he didn't have money to buy food, so he'd obtain raw food from vendors on credit, cook and sell at night to return the money by morning. He continued like that and by two years he'd done well for himself. The last time I spoke with him he told me that he owed none. You have the capacity to build anything you want to build, if you can stop complaining and use the raw materials available to you.

Chapter one

Build That Thing

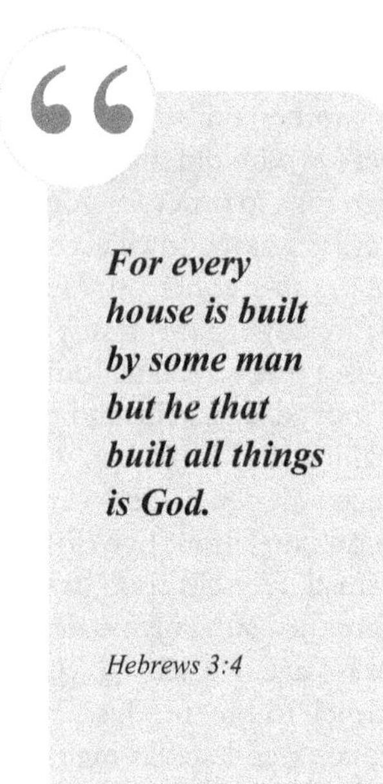

Everybody is building, some are building accidentally, some are building intentionally, and some are building subconsciously. Some are consciously building but the truth is everyone is building something.

Everybody is building something and different people build different things. One person is building a business, someone else is building a career and another person is building a spiritual life, and for another it's a literal building. Somebody else is building his character; know this, **EVERYBODY IS BUILDING SOMETHING.**

We all have one thing in common; we all are builders. Some of us know what we are building; some people are building without even knowing what it is they are building. The truth is that you can build in ignorance. Actually, it's pretty impossible to build being fully aware of what you are building. You cannot build being fully aware of what you are building. A little child that was introduced to a vice at an early age will never know what he is building. Some of the elderly around us are still suffering from what they built ignorantly as children. They were building an attitude; a character flaw and they never knew what they were actually building. Most of the tools that we use to build take time to set but once they set, it takes a lot of energy and work to reverse or change. The word "set" is a Civil Engineering term, when

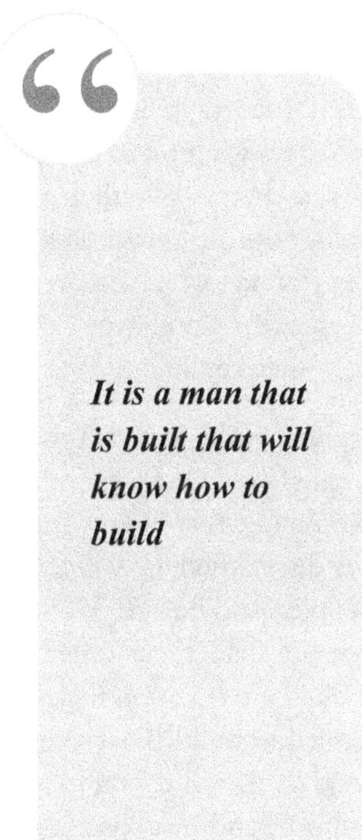

something is not set, you can mould it into any shape you want but once it sets, you can't do anything about it again except destroy it. Cement, once cast sets, rightly molded or not. It takes the shape you gave it intentionally or otherwise. So it is with our lives; once a character sets, it becomes a difficult task to break it. Most times, it takes the intervention of the power of God to break and mould it again. We mustn't all be contractors who work on physical buildings but everyone is building something. You might be building a reputation you don't even know that you are building. Some people have built a reputation of being latecomers so much so that when you hear that Mr. A came, you immediately assume of course that he was late because he has become reputable at lateness. Some people have built a reputation for borrowing and not paying back. Some people have built a reputation for wearing unwashed stockings; and so, have become popular for that, amongst their friends. When such people get to a place where they'll have to take off their shoes, they'll rather not be bothered by their guest. You may mistake that for friendliness or recognition of spiritual authority, but really, a foul spirit is being prevented. Some people are building a reputation of incorrigibility; you cannot correct them, no matter what they do, they cannot say sorry.

We are all building reputations, seriously. Some people are building a reputation of integrity, some a reputation of dependability, some a reputation of honesty. There are people that can be counted to deliver even without any supervision. They are others who have become reputable for literally needing a monitoring chip attached

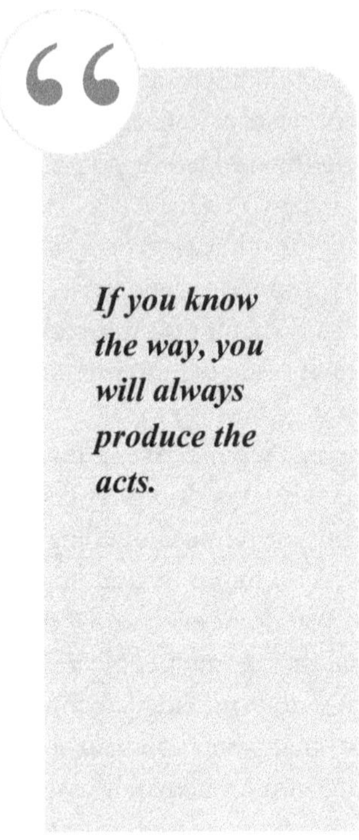

on them to ensure they get your job done. All these are reputations. As a husband or a wife, don't build a reputation for incorrigibility and argument; always wanting to be the man or lady in charge. Whether young or old, poor or rich; it doesn't matter who you are, what you do or what you represent; you have something you are building.

In the business world, it is said that when you satisfy your customer, he will tell two people but when your customer is dissatisfied, he will tell at least 20 people. And before you know it one unsatisfied customer helps you build a reputation that you never intended to build. That's why at every level of your life, you have to be intentional and be conscious of what you are building and how you are building it.

The Bible said, "If we are going to really build something, to do so bearing in mind that there's going to be a storm." If therefore, there is going to be a storm then it matters what we are building on. Every man has a time when what you are building is going to experience storms. Storms come to test if what you are building is solid or not. Challenges are the tests and examinations for the strength of what you are building. Therefore, do not just build;

BUILD WHAT WILL LAST.

God is the ultimate builder but everyone has what he is building in God and for God. To think that what you're building is for you is a wrong notion to have. Nobody actually builds for himself. Every one of us alive is representing either of the kingdom of light or darkness. Whatever you build is being built for what you represent. Look at those that tried building Babel in Genesis 11, what was their crime? God wasn't against them building a city but they said, "let us make a name for ourselves"; that was the problem.

As a believer in Christ, whatever you are building is supposed to be built to make his name great. You don't build for yourself. You build for His glory.

Matt 5:16: " 'Let your light so shine before men'... It's your light. 'That they may see your good works', your good works, but 'praise your father in Heaven'. Now see this! It's your light; your good works but not your praise.

The light is yours. You are the one that discovered where to plug it and it began to shine. Your good works; it's you who sat down to craft that thing; you did the practice, you did the rehearsal, you did the training, you ran the track so many times just to be the champion. He is now saying that when you become the champion, the praise is not yours because we do not have a task to make our name great. He said to Abraham: I will make you; I will make your name great. It is God's duty to make our name great, but the greatness we get from him, comes from the glory we give to him. When we build, we do so to glorify him because in his glory is our glory.

This is how it works; I build for him, he takes the glory, he gives me the ingenuity and idea to build another thing, I get glory, I deflect it to him; He gives me an idea again. I build, I get glory, I give it back to him and in turn, he gives me yet another idea. Before you know it, you have an estate of glory that goes to him. You are enjoying the benefits of the glory. The problem with us most times, is that we want to be seen. No! Our duty is not to show ourselves. Any day you understand this, you will go up without limits.

Any day we understand that what we are doing is not for ourselves, there will be no limits to how far God takes us. Jesus said:

"Everything I do, I do as I see my father do that my father be glorified". That's how it works; you have the certificate, you have the trophy, it is in your house. But he's the one that has the glory. There is a glory that comes with the trophy. That's why I have a problem with anybody that is against tithing. The tithe is not about money, the tithe is about honor. Honor the lord with your tithe. When you give a tithe, its recognition; it's like saying "that I know who does this, it's not my power that did it, and so I am not going to keep everything to myself. I know God is behind this so I give back the honor to him. Tithing is not about money neither is offering; it's about honor.

God was looking for a man after his heart, not for a righteous man, he looked for a God chaser that He'd make righteous. "I fall, but I do not remain there, I get up" these were the thoughts of David's heart. "As the deer pants for the water brooks, so my soul longs after thee". That was what God was actually looking for. He wasn't going to give the kingdom to a man who didn't have a heart that was after him. Because the building of the kingdom is not about the human king, it's about God who makes the king. The building of the company is not about the CEO, it's about the advancement of the kingdom. If you don't understand the "why", you'll miss it. When purpose is not known, abuse is inevitable. When purpose is known, abuse is buried.

The question now is, am I my enemy? So that you don't be like a man that puts his car in reverse and starts struggling to go forward; complaining as he does that the car is not moving forward. You have prayed about village people and it looks like all your village people have died, you even sacked your boss. The new boss still came and the promotion did not come. Are you sure you are not the hindrance? Let him that cleans his house and blames others for making it dirty as he does, remember to check his feet for mud.

What are you actually building? Are you sure you are not building in the morning and crashing what you built in the night? You built it by words, you crashed it by thoughts. He is able to do exceedingly, abundantly above what you ask or think. This means that before God, your prayer and your thoughts are on the same level. He hears your thoughts, the way he hears your words.

We find recorded in the bible that Jesus heard the thoughts of men (Luke 5:18-25). How did he hear their thoughts? Four men were carrying a paralytic and they broke into the house and placed him in front of Jesus. And Jesus looked at the man and said your sins are forgiven. The Pharisees said in their hearts that it's only God that can forgive sins. And Jesus heard their thoughts, and answered their thoughts. He replied to them, "which one is easier? To tell him that his sins are forgiven or to tell him to rise up and walk? They were astonished that he could hear their thoughts. Now before God, your thoughts and your words are the same thing. Be careful what you think after you have finished praying because you can pray positive and think negative. I'll let you answer this; what are you thinking?

> "
>
> ***When we build, we do so to glorify Him because in His glory is our glory.***

When we build, we do so to glorify Him because in His glory is our glory.

The truth is that you can deceive by your words but cannot deceive by your thoughts. This is because man is his thoughts. Warfare doesn't stop with praying, though we walk in the flesh, we do not walk after the flesh for the weapons of our warfare are nor carnal, they are mighty through God, through the pulling down of strongholds, imaginations. Your imagination is a stronghold because the battle is not physical, it's in the mind. If the devil can defeat you in your mind then he doesn't need to war against the physical.

For as he thinketh in his heart, so is he (Proverbs 23:7). You are a product of your thoughts. And God created man and molded man then he breathed into him a living mind (Gen 2:7). You are actually a living mind. You are your mind; that's why in the census, the government does not count mad men because mad men don't have working minds.

WHAT DOES IT MEAN TO BUILD?

Have you realized that we live in a generation where everything is instant? The only thing that is not instant is pregnancy, even with IVF, you carry it for 9 months. We have instant milk, instant noodles, everything is instant. It has even become possible to secure degrees instantly these days; there are now online platforms that let you get certified in your area of interest within a short period of time. One of such platform is Coursera; with Coursera you can have a degree in 3 months and the amazing thing is that companies respect their certificates.

Nobody wants to build anything anymore. Fine artisans don't want to learn how to work. The boy sent to be apprenticed leaves what he came for to observe how his boss counts money. People are sent to learn the mechanic trade so that they can know how to fix cars but they leave learning to fix cars and start learning two things; they start learning how to deceive people and how their bosses count money. Six months later, they break away from their bosses and rent the shops next door only to start destroying people's cars. Nobody wants to learn anything; nobody wants to build. Everywhere these days, you find students who loath reading but dream of passing. Even in basic schools now they arrange for exam malpractice for pupils. What then are we churning out? The society at large is loitered with First class graduates with pass brains.

That's the reason why we don't see lasting private businesses in Nigeria and Africa; nobody sits down to build systems and structures. Most of the businesses we celebrate in Africa that came from abroad are almost 200 years old. We build instant businesses that die with their originators. The idea dies with the owner. This is because we give our children money and fail to teach them how to make money. That's the difference between Moses and the children of Israel. The children of Israel knows the acts of God, but Moses knew His ways. If you know the way, you will always produce the acts. So, how do you build? You build by ways not acts.

What do you teach your children? Teach your children ways. By the time our children come of age, let them start learning things to do; things like photography, sewing, programming and other digital skills etc. Teach them to save, that's how to build. Teach them how to work for money. One of the Bishops I respect in America, Bishop Noel Jones said that while his children were growing up, he would drop them at a hotel to be hotel attendants. Why? To teach them how money is made.

These days, we are producing off-springs that know how to squander and not produce money. But it is a man that is built that will know how to build. This is because as they watch you build; they learn to reproduce the same results. Some of us get angry with our children's teachers when they caution our kids. That's how it starts. One time as a child, my mom came to the school to tell my teacher to deal with me, if I messed up; to grant her license to discipline me. On getting to my school, they both saw themselves and started screaming. It happened that they were classmates from primary school to secondary school.

In front of her my mom said: "He is your son, anything you know I can do to him, do it". That was the beginning of my nightmares in that school. But those nightmares made me see daylight. What some of us that are protecting our children fail to realize is that if they don't pay now, they will pay later.

To build is to make a structure by putting parts together. The question is: "do you know the parts you require to build what you want to build?"

What we call destiny is not far but we branch off to too many places. We spend so much time branching off to too many places.

The more we live, the older we get, there's nothing you can do about that; even If you were to take out the battery from your clock, your time won't stop going. Time does not need your clock to work; your time follows life's time. Crash all the distraction around your life and build a glorious destiny.

Some of us have gathered things that are not even part of what we are building. You know that a lady cannot be your wife, yet you spend three years with her. Three years!!! I remember one old song we used to sing in our old church: "Wasted years, wasted years; oh, how foolish?". You know you cannot marry a man; you know you cannot end up with his kind of person. Yet you say "I cannot leave him, I love him". Oh foolish Galatian! Who has bewitched you?

THE PURPOSE FACTOR | WHAT ARE YOU BUILDING?

The purpose of a thing is the objective for which that thing was made. There exists nothing, without a definite purpose for which that thing was created.

Purpose is that which makes our time here on the ball, juicy and pleasant. A life devoid of purpose is often characterized by frustration and kamikaze living. Purpose is the defining factor in everyday living. It influences our decision-making processes, our relationship choices and of course our very behaviors and conduct. This is because when we all meet in the hall of purpose, each person finds himself rowed into distinct and defined sections because no two people are called to do the same thing, the same way and at the same time and pace.

Living in incognizance about what our purpose is, is the reason why some people seem to be ahead of and above others in life, as entails every sphere and strata of duty. Men of purpose are trail-blazers; they lead the path, wherever they find themselves. Clarity of purpose eliminates delay and frustration. The greatest discovery anyone can ever make on earth, is the discovery of purpose. Who you are and why you're here?

In cases where the purpose of a thing is not known, it would be foolish to assume that it was created without one. From people to things, God made each one with a purpose. For plants it's to be food, herbs etc. for man. For the sun and stars, theirs is to be for signs and seasons. Man is not left out in this; he has his purpose too. My subject of consideration is man, the crown of God's creation. He was not made without a purpose. We find man's purpose clearly stated out in Genesis 1:28.

However, knowing your purpose is not all there is to it. There are factors that accompany purpose to ensure for the fulfillment of one's purpose on earth. Most people stranded in the valley of decision are there because they don't understand their path. If you understand your path, you'd rarely be found in the idle waters of confusion.

PURPOSE AND FOCUS

When you build purposefully, your focus becomes greater. You can hardly drift while building purposefully. When you are building a family purposefully you can hardly drift.

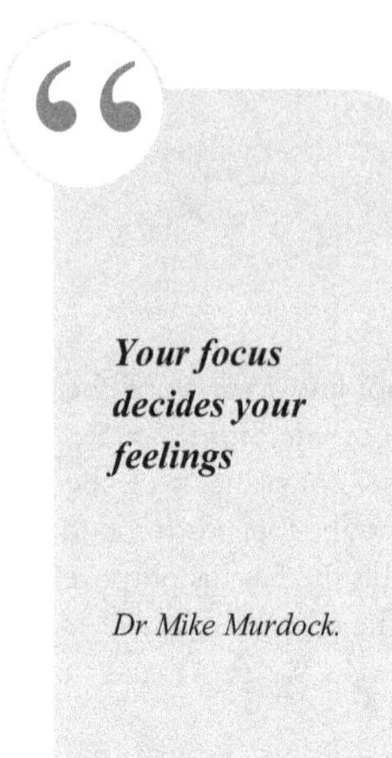

When you are building a career purposefully, you'll be known for thrift and diligence. When you are building a business purposefully, you'll take pleasure in skillful management of resources. Anything that wants to encroach into your capital will be considered toxic. This is because once purpose is defined every other thing falls into place.

What are you building? Some people's prayers have been answered but they are too busy with distractions. The mail man came and dropped the mail in your box but you are too busy with what does not count, that you can't even go to check your mailbox.

This was Jesus' purpose when he came. Pay attention to this;

1 John 3:8: "For this course was the son of God made manifest, so that he will destroy all the works of the devil".

Watch the life of Jesus, everything he did was along that line. For this course you are in school to get a degree and be transformed by the information that you'll gain from schooling; joining a confraternity is not part of it. Hooking up with friends at night when you should be studying is not part of it. For this course you got a job in that office so you can build your career. I am sorry to say that making friends is not part of it. Falling in love is not part of it. When you know what you are building, you will know the things not to build with. When we were building our tent church at one point, the Landlord got confused. He came and asked me, "Pastor, are you building a permanent structure?" I replied "No we are building a tent". In astonishment, he said "okay let me watch until you are done". When we were done, he came to me and said "now I understand, this is an excellent job". When you know what you are building, you will know the things to build with.

When you know what you are building your children into; whether career persons, business moguls, great men and women in ministry etc. you will know what to build with. That's why when two people are being punished in an office; one is sober while the other is nonchalant. Now here's why; the one who cries doesn't want anything to tamper with the career he's building. The other one does not care, anything goes. He just wants his pay at the end of the month; the day the company refuses to pay, he walks away.

The question is, 'do you really know what you are building'?

As a couple, does your family have a vision, do you have a vision for your family'? What do you want your family to be? What do you want your family to look like? Married or not, you should have a plan.

PURPOSE AND INTENTIONALITY | WHY ARE YOU BUILDING WHAT YOU ARE BUILDING?

When purpose is not known, abuse is inevitable. Some young people are into self-abuse? They lie about getting admitted into a higher institution, collect money from their parents for that purpose; the poor folks think their wards are actually schooling and so count the years. This is Self-abuse.

When you sleep with your boss to get a promotion, it is Self-abuse. The Bible says that "the bread of deceit is sweet to a man but afterwards his mouth shall be full with gravel" (Proverbs 20:17). What are you building? Why are you building?

Everyone you see on the face of the Earth is the face of a spiritual force. Everyone you see is advancing a kingdom. Some are doing it intentionally, some others ignorantly; nonetheless, everyone is advancing a kingdom. There is nobody on the face of the earth that is not affected by an influence. Everyone you see is under an influence. Some are intentionally under an influence while some don't even know that they are under an influence. Some people work for devils without knowing it.

Jesus the Christ said, "He that is not for me is against me." (Matthew 12:30). There is no middle ground here. In spiritual matters, you are either here or you are there. The bad news is, you can easily be a casualty by walking in the middle of the road.

This means that at every point of your life, you are actually advancing a kingdom. What makes it very critical is that you are the only Bible someone will ever read in all his life. There are people looking at you now, who may never read another

Bible except you. Whatever you do as a Christian, declares to them how a Christian should live.

As a Christian you don't make a name for yourself. You don't do anything to make a name for yourself. If you died in Christ, you don't have a reputation to protect; a dead man does not protect any reputation. What then do you do? You live for him. He said to Abraham: "I will make you a great nation..........

"(Gen 12:2). If that's his responsibility, then you chill out. It is wise to allow him to make my name great because his scope is bigger than mine. If I want to make my name great now with the help of the internet, with the help of social media to even narrow it down to your city. When you write something and sponsor it whether on Instagram or on Facebook, they'll ask you who your targeted audience is; and their location too. They'll also ask you the geographical locations you want to cover. But when God wants to make your name great, he already told Jeremiah that he is the God of all flesh. So, you actually have a better publicity officer? When God decides to publicize you, not even CNN will come anywhere near the job he'll do. When you begin to build a name for yourself as a Christian you begin to work against yourself. Because every kingdom is run by defined rules and regulations; every kingdom has principles and tenets. In this kingdom he takes the glory. Any day you start to do things to take the glory, that's the day your troubles start. "My glory will I not share with anybody" (Isaiah 42:8). It's an eternal principle. So how do I go up as Christian? It's by defining why I build. What's my purpose? Why am I doing what I am doing? Why do I want to build a great business? Why do I want to get to the top of my career? Why do I want to get to the Zenith of what I am doing?

Why do I want to become a household name in what I do?

Why do we build? The absence of this is why we run around in circles.

PURPOSE AND DISCIPLINE

When you build on purpose, the second thing is that your level of discipline increases. That's why as a student you pay more attention to your studies when it's time to write an exam. Same you that enjoys gallivanting about. Same you that cannot stay at a place for 10 minutes. The same you that skips lectures; the exact same you! When its exam time, that person that cannot sit at a place for 10 minutes will bury himself in his books for 3 hours and leave you wondering what happened to him. This is because the moment purpose is in view; discipline takes its rightful place.

The Bible says that he that is involved in a war does not involve himself in civilian matters (2 Tim 2:4). Have you noticed that when a man shows a girl that the relationship is tending to marriage, she puts herself on an ironing board and makes sure that every line is straight? She knows when to say good morning. She knows when to pass him water; she knows when to call and when not to call. She understands decorum and how to carry herself; particularly when the man has a visiting family member. Why? Because once purpose is in view, discipline shows up. Any day that relationship scatters, she'll reveal who she truly is. Then she'll tell you what she had to deny herself to make that relationship work. You will wonder what she denied herself. At this point you will understand that discipline is not alien to her. But for purpose' sake, for the joy that was set before her, she endured. You could talk to her anyhow and not get any response because there was a target before her.

PURPOSE AND PASSION

When purpose is known, the third thing you'll find is passion and motivation. Take a look at this illustration, a man presumed to lack the ability to save, receives a call from America where the caller tells him that a Lexus SUV 470, 2017 model will be available in the next four months; being an insider, the caller reveals to him that the car costs about 45 million. But assures him that, if he's able to save up 11 million in four months, the brand-new car with a mileage of about 700 miles would be his. I tell you, that same man you think is allergic to saving will not let his one naira fall to the ground until that car has become his. Why? There is a motivation there. Passion drives him.

Let me paint another picture, this is for single brothers that love to impress their partners. You see a young man that hasn't swept his room in a month running around to get his whole house in order just because his date called to tell him that she was on her way. He starts to run around like Tom and Jerry (The popular toon series). That's when you'll know he has the contact of the shops nearby; he orders for an air freshener. That passion's there because there is a purpose.

PURPOSE AND PERSONAL EMPOWERMENT

When purpose is defined, the fourth thing is that there is personal empowerment. You'll find yourself doing some of the things you naturally thought you were incapable of. I realized that these things happen frequently when purpose is in view. Personal empowerment is ignited especially when a person is angered. Have you ever asked someone to help you out with a chore that you were too tired to run and the person started to act up, everyone around knew you were worked up but because the person messed up, you got upset and did the chore yourself? Purpose drove you into doing that; when purpose is defined you start to do some things that you thought naturally, you couldn't do. You'd think some people can't sing until there's a singing competition; amazingly, their frog voices take miraculous textures. Why? A price was staked.

A story was told of a multi billionaire that wanted to give his only daughter out in marriage. He sent out an invitation to all the interested suitors saying: "If you'd like to marry my daughter, come over there's a test". Now, that's one girl that had almost every eye in town on her, so many interested suitors gathered. On that fateful day, the man took them to the pool side and told them that was where the test would happen. When they got to the swimming pool, the man said to them: "the husband of my daughter is the first man to swim from this end of the swimming pool to the other end". The young men thought it was too easy for a test, then came the shocker; just then the man announced that there were crocodiles, sharks and some very deadly sea animals inside the pool. His daughter would be wife to the man who loved her enough to die for her by swimming to the other side. Having said this, the man started walking to the other end of the swimming pool so he could be able to pick the winner there.

While he was on his way, he heard a splash in the pool, and a young man swam fast to the other side. On stepping out from the pool, the billionaire asked the young man "what happened?"; without even giving him a glance, the young man asked, "who pushed me?" Who pushed me? I need to know who pushed me. A lot of the people had left because when the man stated the condition, they didn't want to die for the girl.

But when you are in love you are both blind, deaf, dumb, your heart stops working. It's only a man that is not completely in love that still thinks. People will ask you if you ate something somewhere. As the billionaire went on to congratulate his to-be son in law, the young man retorted, demanding to know still, who pushed him.

By the time they checked, nobody pushed him, passion did. He was so passionate that he didn't remember crocodiles and alligators. PASSION PUSHED HIM!

PURPOSE AND PEACE

There is something else I realized about purpose; when purpose is in place there is peace. You are building but you are at peace, the pressure is there but you are at peace. Everybody knows you are under pressure but you are at peace. Why? Because purpose is defined. When a student is reading a course on purpose, he is so aware that he can't tell you that he/she doesn't know their next step after their one-year service to their country. Purpose is in place.

Usually, you'd often hear an average African man say that he's building for his children. Now that's a bad way to live. Living for your children; that's bad. My dad did not live for me, he claimed to have lived for me; "everything I am saving, I am saving for my children", he'd say. But no, he didn't. The Bible says "a good man leaves an inheritance to his children's children." (Proverbs 13:22) not for his children. Inheritance is not for your children; inheritance is for your children's children. What brought the inheritance is for your children but the inheritance isn't; it's for your children's children. The business and the ways by which you acquired the inheritance, those are for your children. You teach your son how the money is made; you keep the money for your children's children. When you don't teach your son how to make money, he squanders the money that is for his children (read that again).Your son's part is to learn how the business is run; meet your business partners, watch you closely to know how things are done. You don't just force him into the business and assume he'll know what to do. Now note that by "son" I don't mean a male child; your female child can be a son. Look at your children and find the one that's showing interest in what you do. There must be one that has interest, bring that one close and show him. Have the others tell you what they'd want to do. When they do, sort them out. Send them to school to learn that. Make sure they are educated about what they want to do. As for your inheritance sir; that's for your children's children. This is not a culturally-inspired thought-line; this is Bible sense. Even some cultures will wrestle with this. Because the man's sons are waiting for their father to die so they can inherit what he built.

The day your children realize that the wealth you're building is not for them, they will wake up. That's why you see cases where men make money, make names and what have you only for their children to show up out of the blue and tear down everything their father built, in one day. If you build an empire and you don't build succession, you are a complete failure. Success without succession, not just a successor is a failure. If all you have is just a successor, know that anything can happen to him. Don't just have a plan B when English Language has 26 Alphabets; who says you can't have plans B to Z. It's a succession plan, if anything happens to your plan B, is there a plan C, a plan F? Who sustains what you're building? I am talking about building here. So building is not enough. Most of the companies we celebrate in the present day, are from America, from Europe and Asia. Now Asia is taking the third world. Some of those companies are about 200 years old; how did they do it? Look at a company like Kellogg's; you think they started producing in 1981? They started as far back as 1906 in Michigan. Some of these companies we celebrate today were created in the 1600s and 1700s. How did they do it? When they were done building, they built succession. That brings me to my second point. If you want to build you have to plan.

Chapter two

The Planning Factor

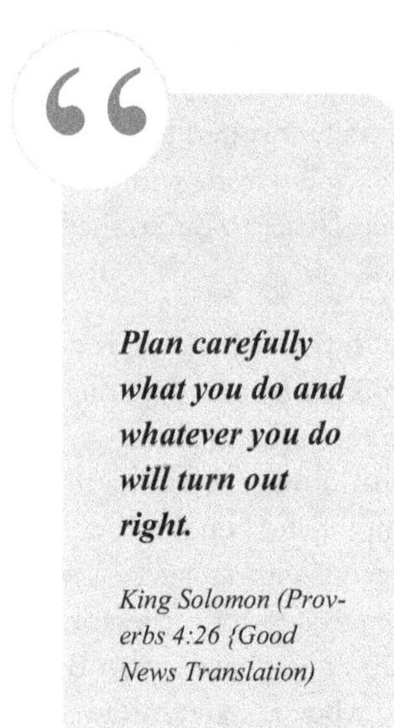

No one builds anything deserving of accolades, without a building plan. Planning simply means prospecting for what you intend to do or achieve. As a student, good grades do not come by accident. Planning, good strategy and hard work gets the deal done for you. Talk about planning; let's consider a few things.

Jesus said in Luke 14:28-32: "Which of you intending to build a tower does not sit down first and count the cost whether he has sufficient to finish it, lest after he has started building, he was not able to finish. Lest happily after he has laid the foundation and is unable to finish it, all that saw him start building will begin to mock him, saying this man began to build, (The problem doesn't actually lie with starting to build) or what king, going to make war against another king, sitteth not down first, and consulteth". Emphasis mine.

See the problem is not building; the problem is sitting down to plan. If you can't sit down you will not be able to stand for a long time. Everyone that really wants to build, sits down first? We are often in too much of a hurry to plan, that's why we fail too soon. The height of a skyscraper is always determined by the depth of the foundation. What plan do you have?

"But, Pastor, sometimes the plan does not work?" you'd say.

Have a plan however. While I was growing up, my dad taught me this; he said "Simdi plan as though there was no God and pray as though there was no plan". 'Planning as though there was no God', this is why some people arguing on social media would frequently say: "see what China is building, is China a Christian country?" 'Planning as though there was no God', that's what they have. But pray as though there was no plan because there will always be the God factor. It does not matter what you think about it, there is still the finger that rules the earth; I don't care what your logic is. If you cannot control a tsunami then that should serve as your reminder that there is a hand holding the world.

A plan is a set of intended action; don't plan if you don't have action in mind.

A lady should be wise enough to ask "where to" when a man shows up and says he wants to go out with her. This is because "out" is not really "out". It could have some other meanings to it... It doesn't make you look desperate. It makes him know you have a plan. If you think you might lose him, lose him. It is better to wait and have a good marriage than to be in haste and waste your time with someone without a plan or worse still, marry a man without a plan.

Planning is the process of thinking about, and organizing the activities, required to achieve a certain goal, there has to be a goal in mind; a defined goal.

How is a goal defined? There has to be a where, when, how and why. If the goal is not defined, it's a wish. You know that if wishes were horses, beggars would ride; you aren't a beggar, so plan.

Let me bring it down to everyday life: You want to start a family, what's your plan? How many children do you want to have? That's why when they ask me when the third child would come; I tell them that I have no plans for a third one.

I am not the only one that was told to be fruitful, I am now fruitful. I add a thermostat to my iron, you know a thermostat regulates. If there are no thermostats there will be no boundaries. I have a control thermostat. In 2001, he gave me the names of my two children and I wrote them down. Charisma, the first one came in 2014. What's the plan? It is one thing for me to have a plan and God changes it; and another thing to not have any.

I will tell him that my plan is for the present two children, if he plans to add any more to them, he'd have to upgrade

If you don't design your own life plan, chances are that you would fall into another man's plan the software. Because I have only made plans are for the two. If you are bringing another two, then get me the capacity and resources to fend for the two; so that the coming one will not suffocate the two I planned for. What plan do you have? "I want three children but my wife wants six"; settle it my friend. You can't build anything successfully or effectively in the absence of a plan. It's like building a house and just adding blocks without a proposed plan; some people's lives are like that. Don't be heavenly conscious and earthly irresponsible. Being born again is not a call to disorganization, organize yourself. Even God, when he wanted to build a temple for himself in the old covenant, he called Moses up to the mountain and gave him a plan. He also said to him, "See, I have given you builders but take this plan and make sure you build according to the plan". Look at the way creation went; you will find from that account too, that God is a planner. Why didn't he create man on the first day? That would have made man the most frustrated being on the face of the Earth. But he created everything man would need first then he brought man.

If you don't design your own life plan, chances are that you would fall into another man's plan

When he brought forth the man, he gave the man a job and then watched to see how he handled the garden. He saw that the man handled the garden well, the man was responsible but the work was almost killing him. "It is not good for this man to be alone," God said. And again, we see planning come to play. He created him, got him busy, saw responsibility before he gave him a wife. Always plan ahead. Don't be that man who doesn't plan.

It was not raining when Noah built the ark. Sometimes when you are building your ark people will call you a foolish man, please don't listen to them. Build your ark. It will rain. It had started raining before Noah became wise in the eyes of the people. Have a plan for your family? Don't be like some of our fathers that trained other people's children and left their own children at the mercy of those they had trained. Plan your life. If you are still in your youth then you are privileged; start now to plan. Are you about to get married? Plan. Plan even if your wedding is still six months away. As intending couples, you don't just plan for the wedding, you plan for marriage too. Don't use all the money you have to wed. After Saturday night, there will be Sunday morning. After feeding people on Saturday night, you will eat breakfast on Sunday. No wedding is better than the other.

Know this: the same people that come for your wedding will forget about it in a week's time and you'll be amazed.

If you don't design your own life plan, chances are that you would fall into another man's plan. If you don't chart your own course you will drive another man's course.

There are three types of planning;

1) **Passive planning:** This type of planning happens when the person in control leaves things in the hands of fate. This kind of planning leaves you unprepared and leaves you at the mercies of whatever life throws at you. The truth is that nothing just happens. I noticed that even the redemption of man was planned by God. That's why Jesus

was called the lamb that was slain before the foundation of the earth. There was a plan.

The people on this lane of thought are those you often find making such misleading statements like; "what will be will be—Que sera, sera"; "if it's going to work, it will work, if not, it won't". Lies! Fat lies, those are. In life, nothing just happens. Things work because we make them work; things work because we think they'll work. "For as he thinketh in his heart……" (Proverbs 23:7)

2) **Panic planning:** These ones are "the fire brigade congregation". They don't plan until there's fire on the mountain. Once, I worked with a boss like that. He'd tell you what will be done in three months' time and when you ask him: "Sir, what do we do now about that? " He'd tell you to not worry because everything was under control. Two weeks to the day, nobody will sleep. "If that thing fails, I will hold you responsible" is what you'd hear. Emotional blackmail, that is. There are people like that; they never make hay while the sun shines. You know if you go to the nearest market to buy an umbrella in

January, average people will call you a fool. This is because it's only January; at this time, harmattan is usually intense. To an average person, it is not raining yet, so why buy an umbrella? But the truth is that you don't buy an umbrella because it is raining, you buy an umbrella to prepare for the rain. You know when Noah was building the ark; they thought him to be a man obsessed with foolishness. According to the scripture, it had not rained before God told him to build an ark. 120 years he was building one ark, that's the whole of Moses' lifetime. Consider from the day he (Moses) was born, put him in the small ark, inside of which he floated on the Nile; till the time he was taken, ate in Pharaoh's palace and ran away to Jethro's house. Up till the time he went back to Egypt and disclosed the mind of God to his people and to Pharaoh, till the time he carried the Israelites out of Egypt, died on the mountain; 120 years. This was how long it took Noah to build an ark. But one day it started raining and all the people that thought he was foolish learnt their lessons, and that, at the most unfortunate of times. Don't let the evil day catch up with you, prepare for it. Will it come? Yes. How will you survive? How do you plan to thrive or succeed? It is by what you are doing now. "Spend as you earn", that's the motto of fools. Please think and build for tomorrow.

People in this category only plan when something happens or when someone is already in trouble. They don't buy umbrellas during the dry season, it's when they go out in the rainy season and it starts raining that they run into the nearest shop around to purchase an umbrella. This is why you'll find a man running around when his wife gives birth as though the child had come by accident. This is a gift that gives you nine months' notice. If you were saving #10,000 monthly, you would have #90,000 by the time of the baby's arrival. If a person hears that you have up to that amount, he can help you with the rest even if it's #200,000. You'll see the man run into the hospital amidst the jubilation of childbirth but doesn't join the celebration properly because there are matters to settle. On seeing his bills, he starts to call on the name of the Lord as though he was hit by a tragedy. He'd been living without a plan for the coming child. Youths with the dream of furthering their education, whose parents obviously cannot foot the bills for such; go about spending any money that enters their pockets. They work and on receiving their pay they go on a spending spree. Yet they proceed to write entrance exams and score high marks. The question now is how do they get in? Often, you'll find these set of people talking about how unfaithful God has been to them.

> **"**
>
> ***Don't just sell for profit; sell to give people as turnovers. When you produce people, you make profit***

3) **Principle-centered planning:** This one is the key to effectiveness. It is the artistically-managed approach to life. It recognizes that life in general can't be graphed on a chart but sees that planning still remains essential. This is one of the things they do for entrepreneurs. When they train entrepreneurs, they give them a plan and they tell them when to plan; it's a straight line, a linear graph. Although you may experience changes in the linear graph as you proceed to work the plan.

Here you consider what's before you and gather yourself. A lot of people are allergic to saving. It started with that wooden safe you couldn't stay faithful to as a child. It started when you wouldn't let the money you put in there mature enough to bear fruits for you. I was of that clique too; I saved for Ice cream—Walls Ice cream. Anytime I wanted some, I'd go and cleverly use a broomstick or something thin enough to get in and out of the small hole of the box to get some Ice cream money out of the safe. If at any point, the usual methods proved futile, I'd break the box, sort myself out, close that ac-count and start saving again. Some people are like that now. They have a Debit card for the same account they opened for their savings, their excuse is that they have self-control. A principle-centered planner says "irrespective of how life handles my plan, I will still have a plan". It is better to be pre-pared and there is no opportunity yet, than to meet an opportunity unprepared. You keep asking God when they'll buy your song all over the world. Now if someone comes out to sponsor and get your song recorded by the next morning, do you have it ready?

Principle centered planning allows us to be flexible without losing focus. Some people become unproductive once they're focused on one thing for too long. Principle centered planning allows us to be flexible without losing focus. It allows us to be creative without losing concentration. Planning is the road map; principle centered planning is the movement. Planning is the idea; principle centered planning is the action. Planning is the paper; principle centered planning is the power.

You have been praying; you want to travel abroad. If someone were to show up now and ask for your passport, do you have one? The thing is, faith without works is dead. It's when you have a passport that even the devil will be surprised. I told myself that I would not drive my Dad's car; I learnt how to drive with my own car; I told myself that! That year, I woke up in January and got myself a driver's license. At a point, my friends mocked me. They mocked that I used the driver's license for cashing checks only. I did not mind but every day I opened my wallet and looked at the license, I'd tell myself that the car was close by, as I diligently worked towards it. That same year, by October I got two cars.

As a student, what grades do you want to come out with? You don't just wake up in your final year, throw your hands up and say, "Lord increase my CGPA." It does not work like that. CGPA is built and planned for from the onset. That you are into ministry while in school is not an excuse for you to come out with a pass. I did ministry in school too, and still came out as best in my class; I was also doing business. If you have a plan, God will help you. Grace works better when you have an edge. What's your plan? The prophecy over your life is that you are ever increasing and ever abounding. The truth remains that God will not increase air. He will not make emptiness abound. What are you putting in his hands to increase and abound?

What plan? No one ever sets out to build without a plan and succeeds. For that which you want to build to be sustained, plans must be in place.

You want to build a wonderful family, what's your plan? You want to build a wonderful business, career, ministry; what's your plan? Where you start is not the problem. What did Jacob leave his Father's house with? What brought the blessing? A plan. When you have a plan, you won't be easily distracted. He came to Laban's house and said he wanted Rachel, they tricked him, he still held on to his plan to have her. What's your plan? When you don't plan, you have already planned to fail. Sometimes you need to call yourself for a meeting. You need to ask yourself questions. How is what I'm doing contributing to where I am going? Don't be that man who others call to help them build their own plans because he has no plan.

While growing up, we all had that friend who was always free to go with you to anywhere you didn't want to go alone. Usually they'd just follow you wherever you wanted to go without asking. Sometimes you both would have almost covered half the distance before they'd ask where you were headed.

Take a critical account of your life, by the time you calculate how many years you have gone without a plan, you'll be shocked at what you'd find. Life is counted in years; it is lived in days. That's why Moses prayed in the 90th Psalm saying: "Lord teach us to number our days". If you don't pay attention to your days you will waste your years. Every African wants to go to America, but there is something called the American dream. What's our African dream? What's our Nigerian dream? What's your personal dream? What's your family dream? It is time to get a plan and work on it.

THREE REASONS PEOPLE NEGLECT PLANNING.

1) Man, naturally does not possess the skill of planning. It is a skill that has to be learned. Some people don't have the innate propensity to drive themselves or project themselves into the future. They were never taught to prioritize. If you cannot prioritize you cannot plan.

2) A lot of people are caught in the tyranny of the urgent. Sometimes you have to refuse to do the urgent because of to-morrow. Have you realized that some of the pressure they put on you to bring money when you didn't have money; you expected the thing to spoil because you didn't have money, yet it didn't spoil; that's what I call the tyranny of the urgent. Have you ever gone to pay for a house only to be told that you'd have to hurry or lose it to someone else? It has happened to me; usually the agent in charge will tell you that there are not less than three people coming to pay for it. In my case, I told the agent to "call them". On one such occasions, my wife and I had already written the check when the man in charge told us that the amount initially agreed to be the payment for two years was now for one year. I asked if he was drunk when we had the initial agreement. He said that there were other people rushing the house. I asked him to give me the check, he did and we left. After one year, eight months, the so-called others, rushing the house didn't take it still. Don't be caught in the tyranny of the urgent.

3) The third reason why people don't plan is because some people don't like the stress of planning. The African uncivilized mind will ask you, "why would you use 5 months to plan for a one-night program?" You call for a planning meeting and nobody will come until it is two weeks to the program, then like bees, they start to throng your phone. The natural man hates planning, and therefore can't come for a planning meeting.

WHY IS PLANNING ESSENTIAL?

We have desires and dreams but "wanting them so bad" has never and will never be a currency for achieving our dreams. The truth is that wanting to have a dream achieved does not make the dream achieved. There has to be a plan. Planning bridges the gap between our desires and dreams, by calling you into action. Planning that calls you into action. Recall that as I earlier mentioned, planning is prospecting for what you intend to do. It is the bridge that leads from dreaming about a desire to actually achieving it.

A wise man said, a goal is a waste of the paper it is written or printed on, until you've started doing something about it. We all have those things we wrote down some years ago that we hoped to achieve. There are proposals we wrote, printed, spiral bound but they never got to the office. So many have thought of a business, registered it and even went as far as getting certified only to go through all these and still do nothing about it. Some even forget why they registered the business in the first place.

THE PEOPLE FACTOR

Mind how you treat people. The greatest power you have on the face of the earth is people.

Let me get to the next factor, we have talked about purpose, we've looked at planning. Now let's talk about people.

People are the greatest assets on the face of the Earth. Human resources are the greatest resources on the face of the Earth. Even God knows this. So, when he even wanted to get the salvation mandate kicked off, he used a man. He became a man because he needed man to get things through to man and for man.

Chinese products are cheap because China is rich in human resources. They sell at a cheap rate because they have a large population. What else will they possibly be doing with 1.3 billion people? People are the most valuable resources in the face of the earth when it comes to building. There was nothing on earth that was not built by people who thought about it. We are getting into the age of robotics; some jobs in the next five—six years will be done by machines. But the truth is that machines will not replace the relevance of people. That's why I urge those willing to listen, to train them-selves into doing things that involve the mind. Things that involve the mind can never be taken by a machine. If you are a pump attendant you need to upscale your skill because in some countries now you don't even need a pump attendant and we are very close to that as a country. This means that with your BVN you can walk into a petrol station, put in your finger print, take 20 liters of petrol and before you drive out of the petrol station, you get a debit alert from your bank.

Banks will have little or no use for tellers because soon what we call ATMs will stand inside the bank to collect money and give out money. It is time to start thinking of how to add more skill to your set. Some businesses are not going to have cashiers, once they have a CEO and an administrator the work gets done. This is because right now, there are electronic ac-counting and audit systems in place—some now exist as mobile applications. All you have to do is type in the details and it will give you an audit report. Meanwhile, some people still carry files around posing as auditors. The truth is that very soon there will be no need for anyone to do that job if a ma-chine can get it done. This is not to get anyone afraid, but for us to see the need for an upgrade in our skill set.

The strength of every institution is people. Therefore, mind how you treat people. Money is not the only capital for business startups, people too are. If you are a producer or a sales-man you don't joke with people. A lot of people that do business and just concentrate on making turnovers don't even do retail, they do wholesale. This is because they understand the place of people and numbers in business. Some years ago, when mobile phones were coming into Nigeria a man brought in a full container-load of phones. He said he brought in about 2 million pieces of phones. He calculated everything it took him to buy and import, and said that the distribution was for South East Nigeria. He said that he made #40 on each phone and in 2 weeks, 2 million pieces of phones were finished. He made 80 million in two weeks. Some of the people that bought those phones were adding #3000 on top of the cost price.

Don't look at the margin, look at the people. When the number of people increases, the margin will increase. Don't just sell for profit; sell to give people as turnovers. When you produce people, you make profit. A fine young man introduced him-self to me some time ago and told me that he had just started a laundry business. So, I gave him some clothes, he returned them and on seeing them, I saw that he did a good job. A wonderful job! He'd just started at that time. What was his drive? I asked. He said what drove him was that he looked for where to do good laundry in the city and he could not find any. He decided to bridge the gap. That's it.

I told him to keep his price moderate and the standard excel-lent, and see how people would rush him. Whatever you are doing, have people in mind. The greatest resource on the earth is people. Mind how you treat people. The greatest power you have on the face of the earth is people. **APPLY CAUTION IN HOW YOU HANDLE MEN.**

Chapter three

The place of intellect and psychological power

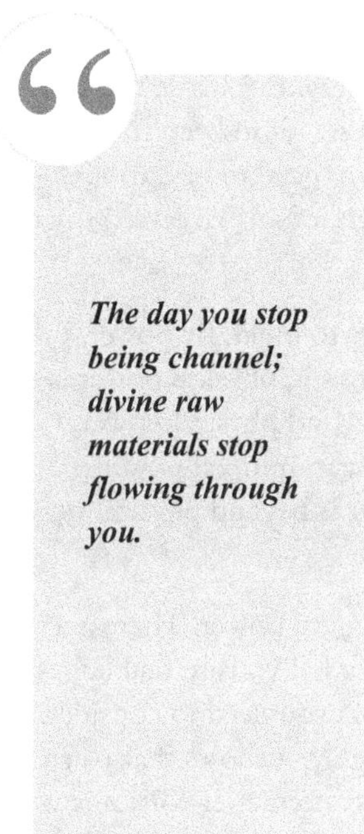

The real builder is not man, this is how the Holy Ghost explained it to me. He said to me: "when you are looking for a house an agent takes you to the house. The agent does everything to make sure you pay for the house; when he's done, you go on to declare your interest in the property and pay. Then he gives you an account that isn't his". "You see," he said to me, "any day you stop understanding that you are my agent building here, I will pick another agent that is better than you. He said I am the builder; you are just an agent. Never claim to be the landlord".

Let me tell you the truth, you're not actually the one building that company. Somebody is building through you. Be-cause that which you are building is someone else's answered prayers. Some hungry person somewhere has prayed to the Lord for a job. When God wants to build a company, he doesn't come to build a company, he puts the idea in the mind of an available man. Now it would be foolish for that man to think that he's the one building the company.

The day you stop being a channel; divine raw materials stop flowing through you. You may be building dear reader, but you are building on God's behalf; that is if you're building anything at all.

The truth is that (it's not the Bible that said it but it is true) an idle man is the devil's workshop. So when you are not building, the devil uses you to build. If what you're building as a student is a good GPA, you are building too. It takes a whole lot to build a good GPA. It takes beyond intelligence; it takes a lot. It takes a lot to build a sustainable relationship. It takes a lot to keep friendships that work. Sometimes to have a friend you need to be a fool. Sometimes to stay married you need to be a fool. You need to take shit and keep moving.

When building, you need so much power to build. By power, I do not talk of physical power. As important as it, physical power is the lowest level of power. Social power is beyond physical power; intellectual power is beyond physical power; spiritual power is beyond physical power; emotional power is beyond physical power. It takes so much power to build.

Let's talk about intellectual and psychological power. There are three things that will determine whether what you are building is going to stand or fall. Three major factors you need to consider. When you consider those things thoroughly, it shows that you are paying attention to what you are building; no matter what it is you are building, whether a career, company, a status or a name. People who are building a status hate having their name dragged in mud because they consider what's at stake. Different people are building different things. Some people are building a career and so, once they sense that a sack letter is coming, they put in a resignation because they don't want anything to dent the reputation that they are building.

Even companies help you to build a reputation these days; they don't write sack letters anymore. They write what they call an "advice to resign". You'll understand this if you work or have worked for a corporate organization. They'll advise you to resign and give you two weeks to think about it. If at the expiration of the two-week ultimatum, they don't hear from you, then they go on to assume that your silence means con-sent. That's when they push the almighty sack letter to you. So people build careers too; but whatever it is you're building, just be sure that you are building intentionally.

There are three things that reveal the strength of what you're building;

1) **CORRIGIBILITY**
Your ability to make changes when you are wrong. As a builder you will make mistakes. No matter how perfect you are; you will make mistakes. The man that will not make mistakes is the one that will not do anything. Once your hands are on deck, they will sometimes pick the wrong things. That's why presently, the industrial world is now resorting to the use of machines. In 15 years' time, most manual jobs will become mechanical; robots will begin to do them. For ex-ample; most developed countries don't need pump attendants anymore. So you'll need to add to your skill if that's all you do for a living. In these countries (the developed ones), gas station services have since switched over to automated means of operation. As a banker, working either as a teller right now or even as a supervisor; you need to start thinking about something else or step up because very soon, the only tellers you'd find in banks are going to be machines. Even your ATMs tell you that cash retract is disabled on the machine; now what it means is that the ATM has the ability to take cash but has been set not to, because it is disabled. Ten, fifteen years from now, you will walk into a banking hall and all you'll see is a mechanically operated banking system. Very soon under-developed countries of the world are going to get poorer because there are recent car engines being produced right now to run on electricity. Tesla's electric motors are but one of such. Just as you have gas stations for gas or petrol. That's the way you will have charging points where you will be able to pay and power your car.

So long as you are building something my friend; your humanity has made enough provisions for mistakes. It is pride; even beyond pride, it is foolish to become offended when you make a mistake and you're corrected. The Bible says that he that is often advised but refuses advice will not find a remedy to his doom when it comes. There's a popular Igbo adage that goes like this: "the ear that refuses to hear will also fall to the ground when the head that bears it is cut off". Some companies that were doing well 20 years ago in Nigeria have folded up now because the people that they placed at the helm of affairs then, refused to change with the changing times.

A friend narrated an event she witnessed to me; a little girl's mother was speaking English and used the pidgin word "gbedu". Her daughter turned and said "mom it's not that, it's this". There was an older person there who had come to shop there too; on hearing this, he turned to the little girl and said "so you're the one now teaching your mother to speak English?" As if knowing how to speak English had anything to do with it. My friend got in the talk and told them not to get angry; "for that right there, is the reason you sent her to school". And immediately she said it, it balanced out.

Sometimes I wonder how incorrigible people can be. As a leader of a group of people; when someone rises up from amongst the people you lead to correct an error you made; please know that it's not weakness to accept the correction.

2) CHOICES

The second thing you need to check is the choices you make. Life is all about choices. "I set before your life and death… "(Deuteronomy 30:19), that's the difference between an animal and a human being. Great choices are products of wonderful options. If you don't have options, you cannot choose. If you are building anything make sure that you have options. What options will do for you is that it will reduce the price, bring you closer to excellence, and bring you to a better frontier to choose from.

You're to wear a green tie to a function; you only have 3 in your wardrobe and green's not one of them. You absolutely cannot pick a green tie because green is not part of your options. Most Africans build mediocre things because there is no excellence in the options. Increase your option. A man that has a wardrobe of about 30 ties, with five differing shades of green will ask which green is referred to; whether lemon green, olive green or sea green or even a sky green if only there was such a thing as a sky green color. Why will the person ask which green is referred to? He has options.

If you are building anything, never assume that what you have is the best. Make sure that you check out options. Sometimes in a bid not to pay more, we pay more. If it is going to take you paying more to get an excellent Job, sir, pay more. In the long run you will have saved money. If you are building a company, don't get used to employing mediocre people and don't get used to paying small money. You cannot build a global brand paying small money. If you pay peanuts you will employ monkeys. Raise the bar for yourself; it will do you good in the long run. What happens when you raise the bar is that it stretches you. Some people show up and when they ask you questions, you'd need to carry out a research on their answers to know them. There's this thing with we African men; an intelligent woman shows up from nowhere and starts to throw intelligent questions then we become aggressive in our ignorance. Don't get angry. It's only a question; provide the answer.

As a parent in this 21st century you need to do a lot of reading and update on yourself because your children will ask you questions. They will ask you very many questions. If Abraham was an African man he would have killed Isaac before they got to the place of the sacrifice. Isaac had come; looked around and saw that the equation was incomplete. So he turned to his father and said: "father here, we have firewood; I see a knife in your hand; and right there I can see fire. So who's the lamb for sacrifice? Abraham being a man exposed to divine knowledge, sourced an answer from the archives of his knowledge of the divine. When Abraham answered he wasn't sure God would provide but he was exposed to divine knowledge.

If what you are building is a spiritual thing, be exposed to divine knowledge. If it is architecture, be exposed to higher architectural knowledge. This is because if you are going to build something that will not be obsolete in the next 30 years, you need to see it beyond 30 years. Don't be too insecure to throw away your options. If you are a leader that is leading a place where artistry is needed be very careful so insecurity will not throw away your options. God will send you men that know those things more than you. It's either you kill the department and be the boss. Or you promote the guy with a higher calling and build the department. Don't ever build only on the options available where you are. If you marry Leah in the night, in the morning you will look for Rachel.

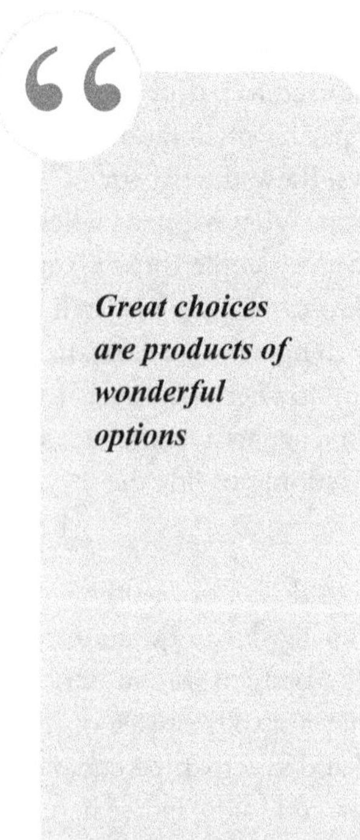

Don't make choices in the dark. If the options are not complete, keep quiet, tell them to give you more time. If they try to rush you into choice making, withdraw. It is better to choose late and choose well than to choose in haste and choose wrongly. It might take you a lifetime to correct. Don't segregate or be too sentimental when you want to choose. If the man due for the job is not part of your clique, do not kill the common interest of what you are building for cliques' or sentiments' sake. Who you're in talking terms with has nothing to do with your targeted income; it's your duty to be matured. While I was in the corporate world, as a sales manager, the guy that made the most money for me was always on my sleeves. He believed he knew better because he had been there for a long time; and so would often challenge and thwart my instructions yet he made the most money. There were sales I couldn't close by myself; I had to send him instead and whenever he went, he delivered.

Such deals wouldn't have pulled through had I sent a mediocre instead; simply because I didn't like the best guy. Don't allow segregation affect your choices; you'd be stupid to do so. When you know the best man on your team, use him irrespective of whatever grievances you have against him. Don't ever swap excellence for sentiment. Get the job done, after the job is done continue the quarrel. The quarrel should not affect your job, when the hammer comes, the hammer will bypass the quarrel.

Embrace opportunities to increase your options, if somebody shows up and says I have a better man for the job you think you are so good at; don't be too insecure to not invite the person. An erstwhile tailor of mine had about four guys that were experts at sewing the bum; he had one person that was good with the body while he handles the neck part. One day I showed up in his shop and I saw a very young lad sewing the neck, so I enquired to know why he let the young boy do the job. His reply was rather astonishing; the young man was handling the neck this time because the young man was a better tailor with necks and collars than he was. The young boy started making clothes as early as 12; his father who was now late, used to be a tailor. I didn't agree with him at first until I sat down to watch the young boy do the magic with one collar and I confirmed for myself. The man was too intelligent to see a boy that was better than him though he was an old man, above 50 years of age then; and not use him for the sake of prospering the business. He further made me understand that the young boy's gift gave him time to supervise general work. Don't throw away opportunities, embrace them. As a wise builder, give opportunities to people that are better than you, let them do what they know to do best. When the praise comes it will come back to you.

Can we learn from God? God is not going to come down here to shine light. See what God said, He said let your light shine before men, they will see your good works and glorify your father in heaven. Be like God.

What makes you a good leader is not your ability to lead well; it's your ability to raise leaders who will lead in your stead as though you were the one, even in your absence. That you are the leader doesn't mean you must be seen all the time. Any day the head attempts to be the leg he will stop being the head.

> "
>
> ***Your thoughts don't follow you, you follow your thoughts; your thoughts create the path and you walk in it consciously or unconsciously.***

The job of the head is to see. As the head coach of a football club; you do not win matches by playing in the game. Don't allow any opportunity to make the right choice to make you feel insecure. You must not do it to take the glory. It is better done when professionals do it. Take for instance, you run a school and a friend of yours is better at Physics while your strength is with Biology; then one day you decide to take the physics class instead because the physics guy was hailed for doing a good job. This right here, is what has killed a lot of departments in so many organizations. This is what's killing my country at the moment; tribalism. If the best is not from a particular tribe, then be rest assured he's getting jumped over.

What do we do with quotas when the world cup comes to us as a nation? If it's only a particular tribe in Nigeria that knows to play football enough to win the world cup then let them go and get the cup for her. When they do, will the cup belong only to that tribe? No! The cup belongs to Nigeria. The glory is a national glory. But the fuss is there because we try to make un-necessary names. Stop trying to make your name great, God has already told you he'll make your name great so re-lax. You are just a cube in a pack, don't try to be the whole pack, you are too small to be the whole pack. Don't build anything on yourself. Build things on systems so that, by the time you step out the system will still be standing.

That's why Bill Gates can say he's no longer part of his company and he is still one of the richest men in the world. Why? He did not build it around himself, he separated Microsoft from himself. It's like God trying to monitor you; monitor your Respiratory sys-tem, digestive system and all. Do you know how many systems that work in your body? Imagine that God had to leave heaven every time to monitor 7 billion people. He only built systems and the systems are running. Be quick to make changes when it's needed. Be courageous to make the right choices even though they are not you…

Make sure you don't do anything without prioritizing. I believe God wants us to build everlasting things; things that will stand the test of time. And if it is going to stand the test of time, delayed gratification is necessary. Stop fanning your ego; it is not necessary. What is necessary is your input. No man has ever built a great company on ego. Don't be too insecure, don't go about saying "it's my company". Any day you start talking like that, you start having problems. You don't need to remind people by saying that. When they wake up and remember your company, they know who the boss is. Give orders; give instructions; take corrections; make changes; increase your options. Increase your options because you can't go global thinking lo-cal. As a man thinketh... Your thoughts don't follow you, you follow your thoughts; your thoughts create the path and you walk in it consciously or unconsciously.

Chapter four

The Process Factor

Process is that distance between the promise and the performance.

The builder, when building, is also built by process. Process is that which builds the builder. As you build, please know that everything you're building will not come up at the same time. Some may need to take different routes in order to get things done. It takes time before any idea comes to reality or into tangibility and the process is that distance between the intangible and tangible. Process is that distance between the promise and the performance. Process is the distance between Egypt and Canaan? Process is that distance between anointing and the day for appointing. Looking at the life of David. He was anointed at 13; at 14, he still walked around like every other person. Anointed but looking like he was forgotten, anointed but not appointed. This is where the builder's capacity is stretched. Most people run away in the middle of the process.

Process is also a revealer of secrets. It's at this point that you get to know who is who. Because as the builder is tested everything around the builder is also tested. When you are going through a test, you are not the only one who'll get to go through that test, your friends also will go through the test. As you go through the test of destiny, the people around you are going to go through the test of trust, faithfulness and dependability. So you get to mark the people that are with you and stay true. These are the people you entrust things in their hands because in the time of process you are easily abandoned, the lily-livered will abandon you, the people that don't understand the vision. That is where you separate comrades from constituents. That's where you separate constituents from confidants.

There are three levels of relationship; they are comrades; constituents; and confidants.

Your comrade is the one that is fighting what you are fighting. You both share a single fight; you have a common enemy. The day the enemy dies, that day your friendship ends.

A constituent is the one with whom you share the same interest. You both met at a job interview; got the job and became friends from then. Your friendship ends the day your interests change.

A confidant is a special one. A confidant does not believe in what you believe he believes in you. If you go down he goes down with you. If you're going up he goes up with you, if you're standing he is standing with you. If you are crying, he is crying with you. He is that one that never leaves. He's that one that stays when everyone else leaves. He is not there because you're a good man. He is there because you are you. When you are bad, he tells you that you are bad. You people will quarrel and he'll still be there, that's a confidant. More often than naught, we take these very rare and special people for granted because they are always there.

One time, I think it was in 2013 or 2014. I was angry about something. I was angry then that when other people disappear, everybody looks for them but nobody checks on me because everybody thinks I'll always be there. I was hurt and felt neglected. They celebrate everybody for coming except I. You'll be well acquainted with this feeling especially as a worker in church; we feel like that sometimes. But one day in the place of prayer the Holy Ghost said to me: "a faithful man doesn't need to be checked on. When you are faithful and people take you for granted it's a sign that you can be depended on".

Sometimes nobody will check on you to see if you came or didn't come because they believe you're going to be there. They'll call everyone but you. The Holy Spirit told me that "when you are dependable, it'll look like people take you for granted. Well the truth is they don't! What happens is that they don't need to check on you because you check on yourself. You are there. You can be depended on".

It may look like everybody is talked about, everybody is celebrated, but you don't need to be celebrated to be you. Just keep being you. Faithfulness is not monitored from the outside, faithfulness is monitored from the inside. It is the faithful that monitors his faithfulness. Any faithfulness that is monitored from the outside is not authentic. Faithfulness is auto-monitored, you do the monitoring.

Have you ever been late for a function and your peace escapes you? Why did you feel that way? Because you are the one checking on your faithfulness. Faithfulness is a fruit of the spirit.

THE POWER FACTOR

Everyone that is building needs power.

You cannot build without energy.

Physics defines energy for us simply as the ability to do work. Most times when we talk about power everyone looks at the muscular structure of the person. But permit me to tell you that the lowest level of power is physical power.

Samson was the strongest man in his day before he died. You would have noticed too, that when they try to portray him as a man of strength, they give him a muscular body? But the truth is, if Samson was that muscular, Delilah would not have asked him: "Where lieth thy power?"

A man that lifted the gate of a city; the Bible said he picked up a gate, carried it up and climbed a hill. If he had muscles, they would not have asked him where lay his power. Was that the case, then the muscles would have been glaring evidence of his strength. It's an argument though; I do think Samson was not muscular as we have been generally made to think. Physical power is the least level of power. I will always say also that the woman is stronger than the man; whether men believe it or not.

A senseless man will always raise his hands to hit a woman at the slightest provocation and claim its strength; that's not strength. A woman can have a sucking child on her back and at the same time, is pregnant; will have food on fire, and will still be busy with laundry while also helping her four year old with homework. At the same time, she's also checking out a Telenovela on ZeeWorld. She coordinates all those things and the food never gets burnt. The clothes are spread and homework gets done.

If you divide those things that she does into two. And give two to a man; it won't take long before he gets dizzy.

A friend of mine once worked with a telecommunications company in Lagos while his wife worked with a bank. They'd both leave for work by 5:00am come back by 9:00pm in the evening and he'd get into the shower, take his bath, get to the sitting room, sit down and doze off. The woman on the other hand would take her bath, enter the kitchen and make ready, what the both of them would eat.

One day while at his place, he confessed to me that the wife was stronger than he was. He'd come in and fall asleep while the woman still prepared, served him food, and cleaned up the place. She'd still wake up in the morning before him; prepare and pack the food that they'd both go to work with.

My friend would wake up, go to the bathroom, take his bath, get in his dry-cleaned shirt; get everything down: get to the car and start to call her down with the car horn. I told him how they needed to improvise if he wanted her to last long. To build anything sustainable, you need power.

Acts 1:8, the Bible says: "You shall receive power, after that, the Holy Ghost is come upon you and you shall be Witnesses unto me in Jerusalem, in Judea and Samaria and unto the uttermost part of the earth."

That word 'power' here, is 'dunamis'; it describes a reservation within us. It's the potential super-ability, resident in us; it's not what is working. No one can tell what you can do seated except by what you've done in the past. But you can't actually tell what a person can do by what they've done. People think they know what you can do because of what they've seen you do. So they mistake your identity. Even your CV is about what you did; when even you don't even know how much you can do.

You will think you can't climb a tall fence until a Rottweiler chases you; then you'll see that abiding in you, is eloping power.

Physical power isn't the only kind of power there is to consider when building; however, it is needful because you need that energy too. You don't want someone gassing out after 3hours for a job that should take 7hours. But beyond physical strength, you need other forms of power too.

That's why in companies, the man that exerted more physical energy earns the least. The one that mans the gate, the messenger the cleaner; they are the ones that earn the least. The MD who rarely sweats is the one that earns the most. Any day that 'the mind' managing the company shuts down, the gateman will not have anyone to open gates for? So that power is beyond physical power?

Jesus now said: Behold, I give unto you power to tread upon snakes and scorpions and over all the power of the enemy and nothing shall by any means hurt you. The major things are the snakes, scorpions and the power of the enemy. When he talked about serpents, what he meant was deceit. If you are going to build, you need to know that you are going to meet deceitful people. You need enough psychological power to handle a con man.

If you are going to build anything sustainable, you need enough cerebral energy to build. The Bible said that the devil sometimes transforms himself into an angel of Light. Sometimes it is not discernment that you need, it is intelligence. I tell people that these days, we are breeding children that are mostly indoor specialists. You know while we were growing up, no matter which side of town you lived in, you had some space for outdoor games. But today you go to some schools and you're wondering where the children play. Most schools around now don't have playgrounds. Those days we had fields. Even if you weren't playing football; you'd surely sweat some by the time you walked from one end of the field to the other end but today, we are breeding more introverted children than extroverts. As a parent, do not let your children be too "soft" that they become butter for people. Let them have a little toughness in them.

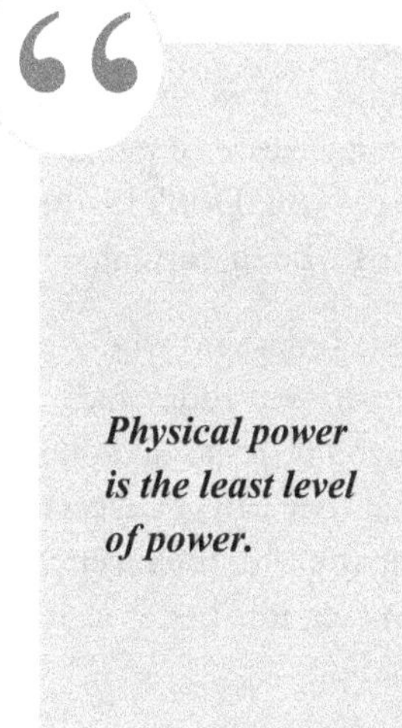

You shall tread upon snakes and serpents and scorpions. But Jesus also told us that he was sending us as sheep among wolves. But instructed us to therefore, be wise as serpents. If you are not as wise as a serpent, you cannot tread on it. Be wise as serpents but don't be as hurting as a scorpion, be harmless like a dove. Know what the serpent knows. There are things grace will not do for you. There are things you need to know.

If as a born-again Christian you have been in the streets, you know those in the street will be afraid of you. Why? Because you know what they know. They will avoid getting in your path because they know you're well acquainted with their tricks.

You need psychological power to deal with a deceiver. What a lot of people call occupation now is deceit, and that industry is making a lot of money. There's so much money in that industry. What do they do? They capitalize on people's ignorance. They capitalize on people's partial knowledge. Don't just have Gnosis, have the epignosis of everything you need. You need to know everything about photography if you are going to build a photography company; you need to know something about everything that concerns photography. So communicating what you want to a photo editor won't be difficult. Because he knows you know what's involved, he won't tamper with your mind. If you're going to build a school, you need to know things about the structure; about building a school; know something about every aspect of the school; know where the books are sold. Don't work like a novice; if you do, you will build a company and die poor; while people will pass through your company and become wealthy. God says "I have given you power to tread upon snakes". One of the characteristic of snakes is that they are always on the ground, but when it's time to bite, their heads come up from the ground. Beware of people that give you false humility every time they see you. Don't let them deceive you with that; see beyond the pretense. Be discerning.

It is discernment that helps you know whose Judas and who's John. When you don't know the difference between Judas and John you'll take the things that should be given to Judas and give to John. Most Judases behave like Johns so that they can get access. Have discernment, don't just run your company with intelligence; it's not enough, education is not enough. In fact, it is better to have revelation than education when you are building.

Try to know the people that are around you. You cannot have authority over who you don't know. Ask questions. As you build, please ask questions.

Sometimes you don't even need to have a reason for asking the question, just ask a question so that you can know the mind of the person. Just show up and bring a question to the table. You can tell a cooked-up story to see how he would handle the issue if he were in your position; then keep quiet and get his response. He will open his mouth and sell himself; get his response pocketed. In that story, you are the boss, he is the person. He won't do anything outside what he said.

Have intellectual power but more so, have discernment power; everything you see on this level is deeper. It's like trying to determine the depth of the ocean by its width. An ocean can be 10000 meters wide but 500,000 meters deep. When I came to the city where I'm pastoring for the first time, the Lord told me as I prayed, not to take things as they appear on the surface. He said: "This city is deep, attack it from there (depth)". After staying two years in the city and running our church 8months in the place, I realized that the city wasn't just deep, the depths are ruled by Darkness; such that the more you go the more light you need. It is suicidal to live in such a place and not have a spiritual anchor. It's suicidal. This is one of those very subtle cities. This city has marine spirits at the peak, yet it's a landlocked area. Just like this city, life is generally deep as well. One of the things my dad did for me, that I will always be grateful for is that while I was still very young; we made ready for school one day as the driver waited. My dad brought me out and told me to look up; the sight was the beautiful sunlight out that morning. I obliged and just looked up for a while. He told me to look on; I wasn't seeing anything besides the brightly burning sun. After a while he said to me " it 's okay you may look down— I did. Then he turned to me and said: "you see how bright and beautiful to behold the sky is?" "Yes" I replied. "The world is deeper than that my son. If you work with anything from face value, you will not amount to anything in life; that is why you need God".

If you are going to build anything, even if you're a student, you want to build a GPA. Let me tell you the truth between the time of writing exams and when the result gets pasted on the board, a lot of spiritual transactions go on. So they make you either pay in cash or with your body.

One of my sons in the Lord came to me one time complaining that he wrote an exam and they said the script was missing. I knew it was something spiritual. I told him go back, that they will find it. At that point it had come to the table of someone that knows what they know. He went back to the same place they told him that the script was lost. They brought out the script and showed him, it's as simple as that. When you know the Dynamics of the spiritual realm, you just give commands, it is that simple. Jesus never sweated to cast out any demon, he knew how to do it. So before he got close, the demon would have already started negotiating because the demon knew it was about to be on its way out.

That is why most men of God on campus come out with the worst results; they are so interested in saving souls that they forget the reason they came to school. These are deep things. You try to build a career and you just wake up one morning to get payed off—you need power.

The fallen man has natural tendencies to wear out; that is why as you age you will deteriorate. If you buy a new car now, it does not get newer. The same way your building ages and starts to look older than it was when you built the house; the fallen man goes that way. But when you understand where you are in Christ you can interchange them. Man shouldn't die ask Biologists; our cells are renewed every day. So why do men die? It's your cells that keep you alive. If your cells are renewed every day then there is a power working out death in us—a power beyond our cells that. It is called the power of the fallen man. You need to stand your ground and make declarations and be watchful. Jesus said watch and pray, don't pray with your eyes closed; be informed. Be informed!

Don't build anything in ignorance; wait instead until you're informed. Don't get into any business that you don't have enough information about. Abraham Lincoln was asked "if you are given 10 years to cut a tree. What are you going to do?" He said he would use seven years to sharpen the knife.

If you are given 10 years from now to cut a tree, you'd relax, you'd say "10 years? That's far! Let me relax for now". But He said he would use seven years to sharpen the knife, looking at him from the standpoint of mediocrity, you'd think him mad. But here is the wisdom; If he sharpens his knife for 7 years, then know for sure that he'd not need up to a year to cut that tree. Add knowledge to your weaponry.

Most times when I talk to people I bring it to reality. These days you find graduates around who take five years to job-hunt; while they receive allowances from their parents. That's sheer folly; but we don't see it that way.

Prepare yourself. It's much better to be over-prepared for the situation than for the situation to meet you unprepared. You over-prepare to get married; you don't get married and then begin to prepare. No! That's why it's "a wife" that gets married; you don't get married and then become "a wife". The bible says it's "he that finds a wife….." ***(Proverbs 18:22)***.

She has to be a wife before she can be found. The man finds "a wife"; so you don't expect to be found if you're not yet a wife. He doesn't find a girl. He finds the one who is over-prepared. Promotion doesn't come to a man that is still below the required level. The man that you see promoted is already above the level, making it only right for him to naturally go up. I am talking about power, I am not talking about spiritual power. I am looking at intellectual power, discernment power. I am looking at information.

Paul writing to Timothy in *2Tim 2:15*, said to him: *"Study to show yourself approved unto God."* Life writes you tests, you need approvals. Some things don't answer to prayer, some things answer to approvals.

Habakkuk said: *"I will stand upon my watch to see what he would say to me and what I will answer when I am reproved" (Habakkuk 2:1)*. Life will give you exams; you need power to finish well.

What are you trying to build? Don't let your case be like that of the Israelites who said in Isaiah 37:3 that they had come to the time to bring forth child but had not strength. Here's a question for you to answer: You have been praying for God to introduce you to the president. And one day by chance you just have two minutes with the president; I mean he gives you two minutes of his time to talk with him. Will you have what to say? Because those opportunities don't come announced. For persons waiting for such a moment of opportunity at this time, do you have what to say? Are you prepared?

The day I met the most influential man in my life. I did not have the slightest hint that I was going to meet him. I just went to see my senior pastor then, and he said "thank God you are dressed well; let's go and see someone". That's why I always tell people around me to always make sure they appear nice at all times. So that you don't need to go home to change for an opportunity, be dressed.

He said follow me. As we started driving towards the environment, I knew something was about to happen in my life. When we met the man, he asked me a question. What do you have to say? I just opened my mouth and let words flow.

He said wait, did you know I was going to ask you a question? I replied "no sir"

He then responded: "How come?" I replied "I am already prepared." I still had more things to tell him but there wasn't much time so requested we go draft a proposal for it. The question he asked me was what he wanted us to do as a company, but he did not want to ask my boss. He thought my boss knew it and his subordinates did not. So he tried me. Thankfully, what he asked was my field and my boss knew nothing about it. How empowered are you?

The first day I spoke on House on the Rock platform. I did not know I was going to speak. It was a training, we were just rounding up service when Pastor Paul—the metropolitan head of the church finished preaching and then said: "Umuahia (my division's location is Umuahia) come!" He didn't tell me what to do, he didn't tell me anything, but I was already informed. So I picked up from where he stopped for about 4 to 5 minutes. Then I concluded service, dropped the microphone, got my pass mark and put it in my pocket. How empowered are you? As a civil engineer, do you know the certifications you need to be an effective civil engineer in this present day? What are you doing about it? As an architect, a master's degree is not enough. We live in the age of professional certification. Where secondary school holders, technicians from Lebanon, just get professionally certified and they come and become your boss—despite your doctorate degree. If you don't know what is obtainable today, you'd be running today with the templates of yesterday. You'd think I will dwell only on spiritual power; but not so. On earth, what we use is the mind.

"Be ye transformed by the renewing of your mind" ***(Romans 12:2).*** *With the mind we serve the Lord. "As a man thinketh…* ***"(Proverbs 23:7).***

"Finally, brethren, whatsoever things are true, whatsoever things are honest, whatsoever things are just, whatsoever things are pure, whatsoever things are lovely, whatsoever things are of good report; if there be any virtue, and if there be any praise, think on these things." ***Philippians 4:8***

"He is able to do exceedingly, abundantly above what you ask or think" ***(Ephesians 3:20).*** Your thinking is at the same level as your prayer. Your thoughts are heard first.

Chapter five

Process is that distance between the promise and the performance.

How God builds

GOD BUILDS FROM HIS MIND

God builds from his mind. He builds as he sees it in his mind. He doesn't build from emptiness because in God's environment there is no emptiness.

In God you cannot find emptiness. Nothingness is inexistent in the presence of God. The presence of God is where God is.

So when God stepped onto the earth he didn't create from nothing, he created from the things already conceived in his mind. When he saw the light, he said it was good. If there was no reference point he would not have said it was good. That means it could have been bad if it didn't match what he had in mind and he would have recreated it.

GOD BUILDS ACCORDING TO PATTERNS

You'd notice if you look carefully in the Bible that there are, prevalent therein, what we call patterns; positive and negative patterns. You look at the life of Abraham, his wife was fair. Isaac's wife was fair, Jacob's love was fair. Abraham lied, Isaac lied, and Jacob was a fraudster. Abraham's wife was barren, Isaac's wife was barren, and Jacob's two wives were barren. Now these are patterns but they are negative patterns.

You find God's pattern when he took Moses up and showed him the tabernacle; he left Moses an instruction and told him to build the tabernacle exactly according to the pattern that was shown to him. Now every time the temple was affected, the children of Israel had to rebuild according to that pattern. You find out every time God was with Israel they won the battle no matter how tough a battle it was; but lost every time he wasn't with them, no matter how weak the enemy was.

We deduce when a person is actually following God's pattern by looking at the word. That is why no prophecy can be higher than the word of God. The word of God is the litmus test for every prophecy. So when the prophecy is not in tandem with the word of God, throw it into the next garbage. Because the word of God is the more sure word of prophecy (2 Peter 1:19). So if the prophecy cannot stand with 'the more sure word' then it is not as strong as you thought.

The Bible says that "Every house is built by some man but he that has built all things is God". That tells you that God has finished building but is still building through man. In eternity there's no time. Time is only an interruption of eternity. In eternity you cannot travel, there is no travelling in eternity. That's why God is Shammah. In God's presence is our yesterday, our today and our tomorrow. That is why when you finish saying prayers you say Amen. You know what Amen means, Amen literally means it is done. So you don't wait until the prayer is answered before you say Amen. This is because in God's realm it's already done. But in your realm, time has to meet eternity, because time travels. That's why my favorite name for the Lord is 'The Omnipresent One'. Omnipresent means that he is at all places at all times but it also means that he is at all times at all times. He's already in 2023 as he is now in 2021; as he is in 2002 AD. God is already there waiting for us to meet him in time. So if you look at all times you will see how God builds; this way you will be able to deduce when someone comes up with gimmicks and some things that contradict God's patterns. Somebody shows me a picture of something that was packaged in a bottle and the person says it's the blood of Jesus;

and that it cleanses us from sin on consumption. That is not a scam that's folly. Now the fool is not the man selling it, the fool is the zombie that buys it. How can somebody sell water to you and tell you that the water will wash away every sin you ever committed, and you gullibly go on to buy that? Yet your bible lies there, dusty in your closets. There are so many things like this; I don't call them deceit, I call them fools selling and the bigger fools buying. Because they are not too technical to decipher—they are not. They tell you that you'll pay a hundred and fifty thousand for them to come to your family house in the village; and that you'd have to fast for 70 days. If you're unable to fast for 70 days, then they'll provide you with people who can fast in your stead for the cheap sum of just #3000 per day. Yet when you meet these self-proclaimed saviors, you wonder who needs deliverance; you or them.

GOD BUILDS WITH HIS WORD

The third way that God builds, which is the more sure way, is that God builds with his word. Heb 1:3: "He sustains all things by the word of his power". I will add, not adding to the scripture but making an elaboration of what was written there; he also built by the power of his word. God builds with his word.

If you look at Genesis chapter 1 you will see a couple of things revealing how he built. If you run a company, gather everyone no matter their qualification; nobody knows what you have in mind; nobody! Every company you see is the result of a fresh idea; fresh ideas birth fresh solutions. Every solution is for something and some people. You will be deceiving yourself if you think that your product is for everybody.

Your product is not and can never be for everybody. I know people who will not use devices made by any other company besides Apple; they'd rather use outdated Apple products than another. You'd wonder if they're in a covenant, neither written, nor spoken with iOS products. There are also other people who no matter what, will never use Apple products; to them Apple products are too selective. But then there are those of us who do not care if it's Apple, Android, Microsoft and what have you? I'll use whichever one can serve as a faithful and effective means to my end. I know one such person—now in the U.S, who will not wear anything short of the designer he patronizes. If you give him any wear that's not his designer's product, he'll give it out. I used to be his size until I grew, he knows i use all specifications; so often I'd check out his wardrobe for whatever I could fit into. When I buy or receive any wear that is his spec, I'd send it to him. These illustrations were instrumental to making my point crystal clear.

Not everybody comes into your company and understands immediately what you're trying to build. As they show up, everything is going to be without form, void and light as was seen in Genesis 1:2. That's why, even as a first class, a multinational company will pick you and still train you.

They don't train you because you are not intelligent. On the contrary! They do that to intelligent people only. They do so in order to harness and funnel your intelligence to the area that best helps them achieve the company's goals. That's how God builds with his word. Before God started working with his hands, he had established everything with his word. The first thing God built with his hand was man. 75% of everything you need to run your company is in your mouth or in information.

Everything is bottled in information, don't ever assume. And God said: "let there be light"; what is light? Light is revelatory information, light is dispelling darkness, light is to make sure that there is photosynthesis and that there will be no void. So the first thing you do is to sit them down and speak what you want. Don't ever assume that they know what to do. Speak what you want. There might be a gas station down the road and you are establishing a gas station. Let your services distinguish you even as your name does. That someone works at some other gas station does not mean he will make a good pump attendant at yours. So sit the person down and find out what you need to know. He may have 20 years' experience, as a pump attendant, do not let that sway you. Tell him that he has 0 years of experience working for you. I have seen people that were teachers in schools and got to other schools only to reveal that there's much work to be done on them. So the first thing you need to do is to speak. Don't run away from darkness, speak to it. There is not a single person who cannot be taught, it depends on who the teacher is and, or on the pace of the person. Some people read and understand; some others only read and understand when they are taught by some certain persons. There are some other people that cannot understand except you paint it as pictures to them; nonetheless, despise no one. Introduce your light; speak!

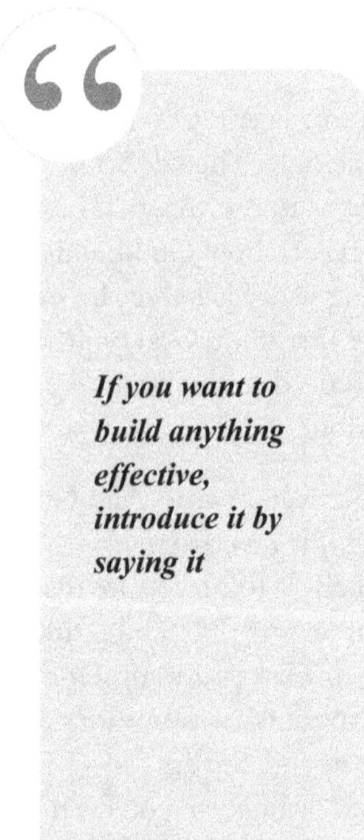

Habakkuk 2:1: "I will stand upon my watch and I will see what he will say unto me". Wasn't he supposed to say that "he'd hear what was said to him"? Habakkuk was a prophet, he didn't hear what was said, and he saw what was said. So whenever God spoke to Habakkuk, he saw. He spoke to Jeremiah, Jeremiah wrote. These are two distinct people. So God spoke to two people, one heard and wrote, the other saw and painted pictures. Make sure you speak. If you want to build anything effective, introduce it by saying it. Some leaders don't speak. Everyone whom God calls to build must loathe fear of confrontations.

Gen 1:4: "And God saw that the light was good and he divided the light from darkness". Immediately you see disparities, separate. Once you have spoken and they are catching it, separate the light from darkness. You don't make people managers simply because they have been in your company for a while. You make people managers because they understand the vision more than everyone else. Growing old is mandatory; as long as they are in your office they are bound to grow old. One day they will wake up and tell you that they have been with you for 11 years. To me that does not count. You can grow old and not grow up; growing up is both optional and intentional. Don't build on age, build on stage. What makes you an elder is not being 85 years old; foolish people grow old too. Not every old man is wise; foolish people don't grow younger. So, differentiate light from darkness.

Let me buttress the point. "He separated the light and called it day, and the darkness he called night". What's the difference between day and night? In the day you see where you are going, in the day you have more help than at night. You'll get more help when you're stranded on the road in the day than you would at night. So, in the day you have speech, light and help. How do you produce the day? You produce the day by speaking. You call forth light and you pick the one that gives you speed. That's why, no matter how much your boss loves you, he'll always choose the guy that's more productive above you.

The light he calls day, why? It gives him speed. An employee may say "Look, my boss prefers the new worker over me and I've been here 7 months". No, it's not done that way. The more light you exhibit; the more chances you have of being in front. When you are light and your light is bright enough to contend with the prevalent darkness ahead; let your hair down my friend. You can only shine. If your camera light is 2.0 Pixel and the newcomer you have trained for only six months has light that's up to 24 pixels. Will you keep him inside the house? Know that as long as you are building anything for God, you are building to have impact. And impact answers to results. So how does God build? He builds with his word.

DEFINE AND DISCRETELY DELEGATE AUTHORITY

Gen 1:6: "And God said let there be firmament in the waters and let the firmament divide the waters from the waters". That is the vision of departments. Let nobody walk into your company and start to assume that he is the head. And because he has access to you, he brings information to you every time; the ones you need to hear, the ones you don't need to hear. There are people like that; as long as they have proximity with the leader, they begin to impose authority on the other people. Make sure that as a leader, you use your mouth to divide the firmament. If you are going to write it as a letter, write it. If you are going to call a meeting, do that. Divide it, let everybody know his place. Where there is no hierarchy there is going to be anarchy.

When things are not divided even the leader begins to walk in error. Like I earlier mentioned, if you are building anything don't be afraid to confront. Because somebody brings more results to your company, ministry or organization does not immune him from lashing.

If there is anybody to even lash, it's the guy with the most results. God builds with his word, he instructs.

***2 Tim 3:16*:** "All scripture is given by the inspiration of God and it is profitable for doctrine, reproof, correction, instruction in righteousness".

There are four ways to speak;

First: You speak to instruct. It's you—whom God gave the vision you are the one with the responsibility of building according to a specified pattern, remember.

"Every house is built by some man, you are the man but he that built all things is God". That means you are getting uploads and downloads from God. You build while he marks what you are building.

"Let your light so shine before men that they may see your good works and glorify your father who is in heaven"

So, what you copy, you paste. If you don't paste on the right board, glory will not go to him and once glory does not go to him, more things will not leave there for you. As the one in front, make sure you instruct.

Also on giving instructions, remember Genesis chapter 1 is the formation of a company, God was trying to form a company. The man that was building was on ground, God was on ground. He was not building by proxy; he was on ground and he was there. When what you are building is at the cradle stage don't ever give instruction from a place from whence you cannot monitor it's undertaking. A lot of people's companies have been hijacked, that's why people that travel abroad most times have matters with their relatives at home.

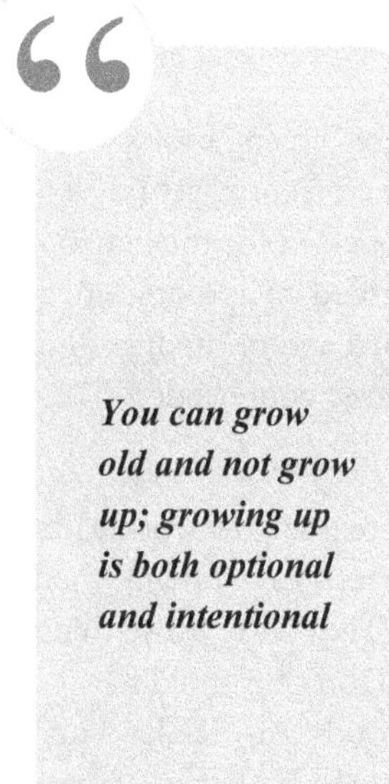

You want to build a structure and on trust, you send money from abroad to them while they send you pictures only for you to come back and find your project undone. Be on ground. A man that is building should be seen where he is building unless of course he has someone trustworthy. And please don't think because someone is family, he/ she can be trusted! People have been more injured by family than outsiders; I say hard things because I am a man of experiences. Sit down and train somebody you can trust, be on ground to build. When you are not on ground and what they have built has already set, it will be more difficult to correct. Don't sell a psychology that you are not there to monitor. Not everyone that said "yes sir" understood you. That's why husbands and wives that stay together understand themselves more than the ones married on Skype. Stay there; don't be too busy for what you are building. God builds with his word. You can attest to the fact that everything I have shown you up till now is the way everyone else builds. But for Christians there is still that part called the God factor, that's why I said Grace works better when you have an edge.

Secondly; you speak to confront. Let nobody under you be too big that you can't even talk to him.

Once, while working with a corporate organization, I had a rep who was working under me; at a time, he started becoming too much so I fired him. He'd counter my instructions to the other reps because he had been there before me, he believed he had the edge of experience over me. He thought he should have been the manager but the organization employed a new manager from outside. It wasn't my fault I was employed as his boss, so I did what bosses do.

He had influence because he had been there 7 years. I took insubordination for a while, called him for a meeting, yet he wouldn't oblige. I called him again and requested for the key to his vehicle; I fired him. He immediately forwarded an apology letter to my desk so I gave him rules; had them typed and printed; got him to sign and I kept it in my drawer. He became cool headed afterwards.

Don't be afraid to confront, because you are going to work with human beings and if you don't guard your territory enough, they will take it from you. How will they do it? They'll say those things you didn't say. God builds with his word. Don't be afraid to confront matters when things start to go south. Any leader who is not able to confront matters will not be able to lead efficiently and effectively. Because sometimes matters will go south. People are going to do what they thought was good, not what was on the template; they don't do this necessarily because they're bad. They do it most times because to them, it's what should be done. But the truth about it is that what's good in their eyes will not always be good for the assignment. I will put it like this. It might be good but still not right. One of the things that have spoiled the things that men have built particularly in Africa is sincerity.

Does it mean we should not be sincere? No, be sincere! But don't stop at being sincere. You can be sincere and sincerely wrong. Be sincere; but at what you are supposed to do. Be honest but know your boundaries. You are sincerely trying to bring in another man's vision into what another person is building and the man building says it's not necessary; don't get upset; accept it. Don't say this is how it works in other organizations; No. That is one thing that will kill your organization; bringing in something from another organization that looks like your own into your organization because it works for others.

That's why we have DHL, UPS, and EMS. They're all courier services. Some people use any courier services while some others have never set foot in a UPS office. The reason they are different is because they all sell distinct characters, there is an attitude they sell. That is why irrespective of how some company's logistics upset their customers, they never leave; why? The brand has successfully sketched their quality upon her customers' very being. If what you are building is different; be confrontational. Attack what is not it. Let them know it's not what you are building.

It's like a man that goes to inspect his house under construction only to get there and see a pillar where there should be no pillar according to the building plan. If he keeps quiet be sure then that he'll get something that's not part of the plan. Be vigorous; tell them to pull it down. Of course, they'll make excuses; they will say this pillar is going to help. But you insist that it is pulled down because it is not in the plan.

Thirdly; you speak to ask for feedback. Hebrews 1:3 says "and he sustains it". Always ask for feedback. Anybody that tampers with feedback will not help what you're building. Because most of the things you don't even know will show up in feedback. Most of the things they will tell you in words will not tally with your binoculars; you will not see them. But by the time they bring feedback, you will be able to adjust. There are some things God has been able to reveal to me about the church I pastor as a result of feedback. Ask for feedback. Before God created the next thing, he made sure that the one he was onto was good. So, he got feedback, tied it up and went on to the next thing.

> ***The more light you exhibit; the more chances you have of being in front.***

Many times, people will come to ask me "pastor, why are we not doing this? And every time my response has always been "wait it's not time". Don't ever hurry to impress anybody unless you are not building a long-lasting organization or structure. If you are going to build anything that will outlast you, stay put, and watch your time. Confront what you need to confront. One of the leadership qualities I find and respect in my wife is that she knows how to confront me. You told me that this is where we are going, why are we taking this path? She'd ask. And if my explanation is not concrete, we'd have to scatter and go back to the path. If the explanation is satisfactory, we continue because she knows I know what I am doing. Ask for feedback.

God took time and departmentalized everything. Watch it, let it be the way you put it. The Bible says he sustains all things by the word of his power. It is one thing for him to source it; it is another thing for him to sustain it. Ask for feedback, go back and check, don't just relax. If you want to build anything that'd last, make sure you go back and check even if you don't trust the person. Have Fellowship with them.

I believe that when Adam still had fellowship with God in the cool of the evening, a part of the fellowship that God had with Adam was feedback. How did today go?

How is the department working? How are you coping? Go for feedbacks.

And fourthly; you speak to correct where necessary, and do so without fear.

You are a new creation and you are a speaking spirit. You get into your closet and you bring that company and put your breath on it. Matters will begin to arise in the place. Speak what you want. God saw what he said. You can train people and they will do the wrong thing but you cannot speak life to the company and it will produce death.

Study all the management books you can lay hands on but know that there's still what is called "the finger of God" in your company.

Duet 8:18: "It is the Lord that gives us the power to make wealth". Because what creates wealth is what created the world. I call it "Elohistic tendencies", he put them in you. The things Elohim did in Genesis you can do now in 2021. Is the business not producing as it ought to? Wake up early in the morning, bring the business, call it by name, and say "let there be profit in this business".

Speaking spirits cannot but see what they have spoken though it wasn't the mortal that spoke. Before you speak to the people, speak to the business so that the business will not repel them. That which you are building as long as it's growing, is a living thing. If it is a living thing, then it hears. You should give instructions to everything that hears around your environment. That's why when you want to register the company, they ask for the name; this means it can be identified. Anything that has a name can be identified both in the natural and in the spirit. So call it by name.

Last year you didn't do well, speak to the New Year. Tell it what it's going to give you; give it a defined expected turnover. Be confrontational. When I talk about our church, I speak as one without senses; but before us, everything said is happening, one after the other. Not because there are finances, no. God created the word before money came. Elohim does not need money to create, even money was created. The world was already in existence before money came. So "no money" is not an excuse for not building. There are things money can buy, but the costliest of things that you need to build are those things money cannot buy. Speak! Call forth! You don't have money to pay for a professional, call him forth. A professional can show up from nowhere to volunteer for you; seeing that what you're building is a global one, then he decides to be part of your cradle days. Did you pay him? No, you called him forth. We have the power to call forth.

I will not pay for what grace can pay for; I will call it forth and once it shows up, grace will pay for it. The ones that don't show up I will pay for. Once I need something, I ask; "lord this is coming". "Lord, I don't want to trek anymore; I feel my car is coming". The words I speak are spirit.

One time my car was faulty so my wife and I were left with just

a car. I had to go where I didn't plan to because I had to drop her off. I woke up tired of the situation one day and prayed "Lord I am tired! I need my car fixed but I don't have money to fix the car". Not too long after, someone showed up at my house, and asked "pastor what we are doing with the car?" I didn't tell him anything. He asked me why I wouldn't fix the car; I told him I didn't have money to fix it. Immediately he asked for the keys, left with the car and brought it back fixed.

I didn't give him a penny; he fixed it, brought it back and kept it in my house. He spent over a #100,000 fixing the car and he didn't want me to pay anything. For integrity's sake, I paid him back as soon as I had cash to do so. Now that is beyond money.

You can call jobs, "……calleth the things which be not" ***(Romans 4:17).*** "Be not" means be not, don't put boundaries on it. Everything we have in our church is church property, none was borrowed; we called them forth. If it worked for us, it will work for you.

They told you it's impossible to make 1million in your first year in business. Now who told you that? Who put the rule there? You can do your first deal and get a turnover of 35 million. How does God create, he uses his word. We have used so much sense that we have become cautious enough to only speak in tongues in church. Tongues in church are for our tanks' refilling.

The capacity of the car is not known at the gas station, it is known at the express. When you are done filling up in church then my friend, get on the express! The Bible said when they (the church at the upper room on the day of Pentecost) spoke the people heard them. Let your company speak in tongues by the profit you declare at the end of the year God used 5 days to create everything we see and everything we don't see. Your life is not a project; six months is too much.

God can turn things for you in a moment.

The man Joseph slept as a prisoner one day and by the next day, he slept in the palace having access to whatever he wanted. God builds with his word; don't joke with the words you say. Every idle word that man speaks he will give account (Matthew 12:36); there are no idle words.

GOD BUILDS FROM HIS MIND

Anyone willing to build any lasting structure must know how to speak. You can't be a great leader if you don't know how to communicate.

In Genesis 11 they were unified in speech. When God wanted to affect them, he affected their speech. The project died when he gave them various languages. That tower was never built; actually, that tower never rose. The Bible says that they had only imagined building; that means they did not actually build. We were told that they built to a point, and God scattered it; on the contrary, they didn't actually build. They were still imagining. The Bible says that

"that which they had imagined to build, none would have been able to stop them". What this is saying by implication is that building starts first in the mind.

The greatest nation on the surface of the earth is not the USA. The greatest nation is called the imagine-nation. In your imagination you can live anywhere, you can go anywhere. In your imagination there are no boundaries; the customs cannot stop you. You can be the king, the president, the policeman, nobody will stop you.

Writing the vision is not enough, you can write the vision and nobody will understand what you wrote. He (God) also told Habakkuk to make it plain upon tablets (Habakkuk 2:2); not one tablet but "tablets", write it in a way that it will be easily understood by anyone—even a lay reader; make it plain to an extent that even a child will understand what you want to do—peradventure you need a child to be involved in it. Make sure that you are not afraid to speak.

GOD GETS ACTIVELY INVOLVED WHEN HE BUILDS

The next thing is that when God builds, he takes action. Taking a look at the creation account, you will realize that Genesis 1 was just "talks". When he got down to Chapter 2, he bent down and began to work. The spirit man was not formed, the spirit man was spoken into being. But when it was time for him to transport the spirit man from the spirit to the physical realm; he got to work. Anyone that wants to build anything should be on the ground to work. People don't really listen to what you say. People see what you do. If you want to build a family, you don't build family by instructions, you do by examples. Your children see you more than they hear you. Even the people that God sends to work with you, they see you more than they hear you. If you say that your resumption time is 8am, Sir, please as long as that office is still in its cradle stage; be in that office way before 8am. If you talk about accountability then be the example. If you say dress properly, let them understand it by looking at you. God after talking, got his hand dirty with dust; from which he made man. There are tasks that you don't delegate.

Any man that is building has to know everything about what he is building. I walked into church one evening and found out that something was wrong with our sound system even though it seemed normal; I was able to know this because it's important to know something about everything. A time will come in the building process when you'll be left alone and still be expected to deliver. At that time what will you do? So many parents do not know how to bathe their children because there's a nanny to do it. Should the day come when your nanny is incapacitated; will your children go to bed dirty? You have to know how to do it. Be the first example of what you pay people to do for you. Know something about it. God said, come and he began to form. There was something in his mind; he formed that thing first. And every other thing being formed is drawn from that.

People that make clones now take clues from what God formed. But God had a mentee called Adam. Adam was with him when he finished forming what was in his mind and planted the garden. That was another thing God did with his hand. To plant means he took seeds and had them put in the ground. Don't read the Bible from an abstract view. And when he was done planting the garden, he took Adam and planted (put) him there. This means that Adam was there with him, observing as God planted the garden. He would have planted the garden before he made Adam; but he formed Adam first and had him watch as he planted the garden; he was already a living soul. The next thing God did was that he instructed Adam to dress and keep it. Most times we give instructions to people that don't even see us work. The truth is that a lazy builder cannot build workaholics. If you are a lazy lecturer your students will not take you seriously.

You fix lectures for 7:30 and by 9:30 no student shows up because they know you won't even have arrived by then. Whoever builds, let him build by examples; what examples? Remember where we started. I said people build intentionally while others build without knowing that they are building. When you're done speaking and making utterances, bend down and build. The things you have in your head should come on paper too. The things you have on paper should be on the ground too as they're on paper.

As a student that wants to build a reading culture, what do you do? First you bring it from your head down to paper; you create a timetable. You map out say 7:30pm till 10pm for study. But after three weeks, the study time becomes TV time.

The initial plan of reducing your exams' workload becomes

a defeated one. By the time your exams period comes, you're forced to read all night. Because what you don't build intentionally, pressure will make you build. If you don't build a good reputation, pressure will make you build one; you will try hard to save face. Everyone, in whose heart God had put a purpose, has work to do.

Chapter Six

B---Bravery

To further break down the many ways we can get our hands on the ground for action, we'll be looking at the word BUILD acronymically.

To be brave means to possess or exhibit courage or courageous endurance in the face of fearful circumstances. Anybody that wants to build anything should get ready to be challenged. Life answers to the brave, if you want to build anything lasting, get brave; be brave. Joshua was about to take over from Moses. Moses was dead and the only thing God told Joshua was to be courageous. God told it to him three times from Joshua 1:7-9. God told him that he wanted to build a nation with him; and that he was going to be challenged.

Habakkuk put it like this: "That I might know what to answer when I am reproved". You will be challenged; will it break? Yes, it will! Should you pick yourself up when it does? Absolutely! Because staying down means what you need to build will not be built. To be brave is to have an encounter with courage and fortitude. What does it mean to encounter? It is to engage face to face; to engage in conflict as with an enemy. Anybody that wants to build anything new will have to face new devils. If you are going to build something, you have to face new devils. One of the greatest devils you are going to face is called "we've never done it this way". It is worse in church; they will even spiritualize it and tell you that God does not move like that. They will say this cannot be God". I remember when we bought a set of drums for the first time in my maiden church. She was one of the first churches to buy a set of drums back in those days. I remember when the drums arrived in church; we—as children, were very happy because those of us who were privileged to have had television sets back then, recognized it from what we saw on T.V. Here it was; what we're seeing on TV was right in front of us and we had somebody in church who could play; it was just wonderful. So, the drummer got playing. He was playing it until one of the deacons showed up and said that drums were made for night clubs. That this could in no way introduce the move of God; instead as he claimed, it would make the youths to start visiting the night clubs. The use of the drums was thereafter suspended for one year; now forward to today, does it enhance worship? Yes! You'd agree with me that it would make you sick to step into a church today for Sunday worship and learn that you're only allowed to clap as a way of celebrating the Lordship of Jesus. Most times, the generation present with you will not understand what God will commission you to build. If they understand it, it would not make news, that's why it's new. What is news? News is just new with an "s". If you listen to the news and it's not new, it is no longer news. Some things that others consider news is not news to you, why? You have heard it before. So, news is plural of new. God wants to use you to make news. That's why he is putting new things in your mind but you have to be brave to build it.

The greatest threat to transition is tradition. Tradition is as evil as religion, just that religion uses God to perpetrate evil. How will our world be without twins? Imagine there were no twins in the world today. Some years back tradition killed twins. I remember also, the very first time the youth choir wanted to host a music concert in my maiden church. One of the elders called me and said "Chisimdi! So, you people want to bring the world into the church?" Back then, there were no LED lights, so we improvised, we used Halogen lamps. We wanted to mirror the same effects we saw at concerts hosted by great gospel artists of that time—Ron Kenoly and Don Moen. We saw different shades of light. In our little minds we thought that they'd simply used painted halogen lamps; we wanted to have the same effect.

We got brand new halogen lamps; painted them with different colors and installed them. One elder walked into church after we finished the battle and immediately the man walked into the church and saw different colors of light he screamed: "the blood of Jesus". The issue became a problem because from where he was at that time, he couldn't understand what drove us. There was a yearning; our minds sought for 2019 in 1999. The first time someone told my uncle that he was a blogger; my uncle's response to him was that he was jobless. Today everybody is a blogger, even people that struggle with spellings.

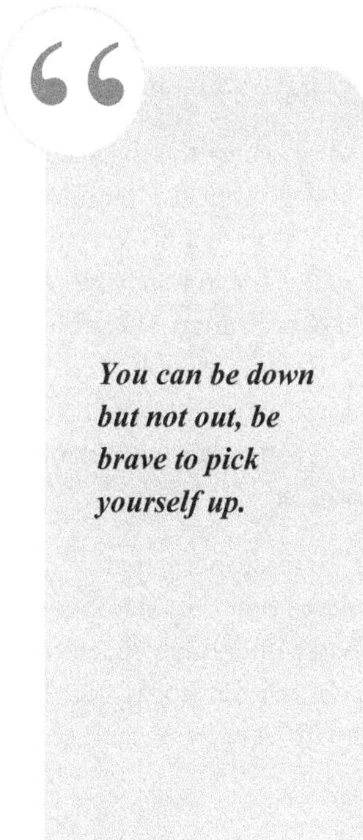

That they do not appreciate it doesn't mean it won't sell. The Bible says: "Heaven rejoices when one soul gets saved" what this means is that even 1% is enough as long as it's the will of God. A major evangelist organized a crusade, some 110 years ago; had it publicized. People told him that nobody had ever done a crusade there and he told them that it was God that told him to do it. However, everybody he had expected for the crusade did not come, excepting a little boy that came on the third day. On that day, the evangelist preached the way he preached on the first and second days. The boy got saved, he led the boy to Christ. The lad came back again the next day which was the last day of the crusade. After the man of God had finished preaching, to a crowd of empty chairs, he went back to God and asked: "God why did you send me to disgrace myself"; the lad that got saved was surely not an encouragement.

When he enquired, the Holy Spirit told him that the crusade was a huge success. He wondered how, because one minor got saved? Many years later, the young lad that got saved in that crusade became the highest recorded soul winner ever. He was Billy Graham. To the man that followed God, the crusade was a failure. Many years later from then the crusade turned out a massive success after all. Some of the things God is putting in your heart right now to build are so weird that even your father calls you a fool; build nonetheless. Take the bull by the horn, be brave about it.

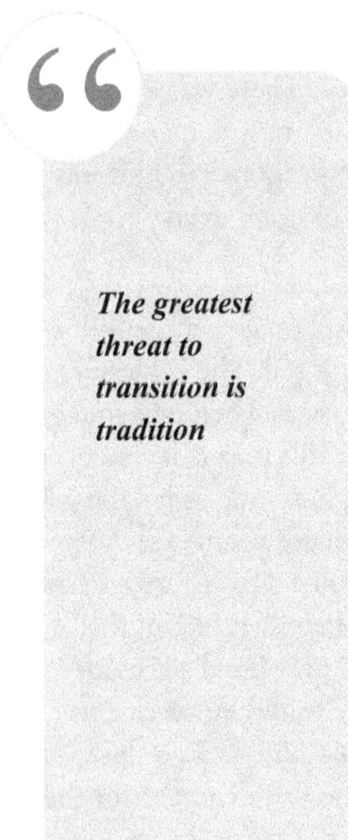

I realized that most of the marriages that thrive and do well are the ones that encounter storms at its very first stage. You will want to marry her and they say you cannot marry her. They give you excuse like "people from that town don't marry from our town". Put your hands to work and be brave about it.

To be brave means to defy any challenge. I remember when we were getting into our tent church; they told us that they'd not give us the space. Their reason was that they had not enough space for us. We wanted the warehouse beside the church but it was full. The lawyer showed us a space heavily trashed with very heavy and old equipment.

When I saw the space, I got very discouraged. "They could have just told me they had no place for us instead of mocking us", was what I muttered angrily to myself. I told my wife that we were not going to wash our linen outside here, so that God could move us out of here as quickly as he can. When I got home and prayed,

God told me that this was the place to start; "which place?" I asked.

When we decided to take the place, they told us we would need a crane to move the equipment. One of us suggested we use a Hiab crane; which is very expensive. We found an operator and he charged us #250, 000. I told him that he was just moving the equipment, not the foundation. As I was talking to him, he was leaving the place. I called him back and told me he'd do the job only after he had returned from his holiday trip; it was still 2nd January. I went in search of another operator, that one charged us #300,000. I went back to God complaining about how impossible the whole situation was looking; I said "Lord do you see?"

We finally found someone who agreed to do the job for #200,000; he came into this place and worked for 5 days and wouldn't continue till we talked about money. We finished building and on the 10th of February, I announced to the church that we'd be moving out of the hotel; everywhere got loud. I announced that by Monday evening we would start prayer meetings at the just completed site. We came and after our prayer meeting it began to rain, we realized that they didn't tension the tent and so, it started to sag. We tried to contain it and then agreed that by the next day, they would come to fix it. 7:30am the next morning, I got a distress call from one of us, beckoning me to come to the site. I asked him what happened and he wouldn't budge; he insisted I come so I obliged. I got to the site to see that everything we built had collapsed; everything.

You have to be brave because sometimes when you finish building, you might wake up one morning to see everything you built on the floor. I walked into the place and cried like a child. I asked the Lord why he had to bring me here only to disgrace me. Most times in life your courage to build will be tested. To conquer is to rebuild what was built that has fallen. What did you build that has fallen friend? Was it a relationship and it scattered? Build another. Did you build a family and it looks as if it is falling apart? Rebuild it. As for my story, we picked up the tent but first, I picked myself up.

The same people that saw me that morning came back by evening and couldn't believe I was the same person. Because I had picked myself up by the time they got back.

Life will knock you out, but it's your job to determine whether it's a knockout or just a fall. You can be down but not out, be brave to pick yourself up. Theologians told us that the earth of Genesis chapter 1 verse 1 was a perfect earth. But between verse 1 and 2 what God built scattered, from verse 2 God had to start rebuilding. If what God built can be scattered, then it just leaves the hands of the person to another person because visions are eternal.

Where there is no vision, the people perish but when there are no people, the vision does not perish; it just leaves the hands of the person to another person because visions are eternal.

Listen to me, visions don't die. Where there is no vision, the people perish but when there are no people, the vision does not perish; it just leaves the hands of the person to another person because visions are eternal. It's painful to wake up one day and find out that someone else has built and is reaping dividends from the same thing God gave you to build fifteen years ago; because you chickened out. Have you ever walked into an office and it looks like what you saw in your dream? Has somebody ever shared an idea with you and it looked like what God told you four years ago? Has someone ever come to you wanting to sell a product to you and you realize that someone else brought the same thing to you 3 years ago?

Be brave to build that which God has called you to build. Will there be challenges? Yes. But will you build it?

Yes. Will it scatter? Yes, it may! Will you build it? Yes, you will. At a point in my life I said that I was not going to get married anymore. You too may be at that point now; but like me, you too will get married. Did they break your heart? They broke mine too; go and pick it up from whence they broke it and move on. I hear some ladies say that "all men are the same". In truth this would mean you've tested them all. Such pseudo-statements as "all women are the same", "men are dogs". It was your ex that was a dog, not all men. Not all men are dogs; the one whose words you read now is not. This disproves you of your psychology and philosophy. Sit down and be a wife, the right man will find you. I realized that physically, like terms repel. But spiritually, like-terms attract. If you find yourself attracted to a kind of man and a kind of woman; then check yourself. I realized that it only takes smokers three weeks in a new area to connect with like-minded people. Because like-terms in the soul attract. If you always attract prostitutes; check yourself for immoral tendencies. After all, prostitution is not relegated only to females.

Chapter Seven

U—Understanding

When you know your identity you will know your position. When you know your position you will be able to embrace your reality.

As one building, you need to apprehend and be in full comprehension of so many factors that play vital roles in your assignment. That is what understanding is all about. It is having a mental grasp and full comprehension of what you're dealing with.

There are certain factors you must come into cognizance of as you build. Paying less or no attention to them could mean peril to you and to your purpose. Therefore I urge that you treat as expedient, the following;

UNDERSTANDING YOUR STRENGTH AND WEAKNESS

When you understand them you will be able to spot your opportunities and your threats. When you know your identity you will know your position. When you know your position you will be able to embrace your reality.

UNDERSTAND WHO YOUR ADVERSARY IS

You also need to understand your adversary; know who your enemy is. It is intelligence to know who is not with you. It helps you to do things right. It helps you to put your foot in the right places while you build. Not everybody is happy with what you are building. Our main enemy is the devil but sometimes the devil is not always the problem; sometimes it is you.

Be careful not to be the weapon that is fashioned against yourself. You see, the enemy that affects you the most is the enemy you like. The devil will never tempt you with what you don't like. So don't go bragging about how you didn't fall into fornication. Fornication was not your fancy. Where you are standing another falls, where you are falling another is standing. So don't claim to be superman in another person's idiosyncratic weak point; truth is you have yours as well.

James the Apostle put it this way: we are tempted, enticed and drawn away by our own Lust (James 1:14). Anything that does not appeal to you cannot be used to get you. If it's a chubby woman that appeals to you, he will not bring a slim woman. He will always bring that one that is the flint to your fire. So you need to understand what or who your enemy is. I prayed that prayer; I said "lord deliver me from the enemy I like. Save me from that enemy that will be my undoing; whom I find it hard to let go".

I had a boss, to whom his account handler was dishing mayhem. He knew what was happening; he believed that things wouldn't go right should he let the man go. When he finally let him off, too much damage had already been done. This actually goes beyond character; it reaches to you and to the person, and also the devil. As a builder, extravagance is an enemy.

UNDERSTAND WHO YOU ARE BUILDING WITH

You need to understand who you are building with in order to know what to commit to their hand. As an employee you need to understand your boss; know when to talk to him and when not to. If you are building a family, understand your partner; this may take a long time but make extra effort to do that. It will save you a lot of energy.

According to their position in your life, whether up there, down there or besides you; seek to understand them. Up there is your boss, down there is your subordinate, and by your side is your partner; for those people building a family or a partnership.

Understand who your partner is. If your partner is the type that does not keep to their word, don't do anything without writing it down. Don't say "I trust him"—sometimes trust is proven when it is written. You like him but you can't trust him if he's the type that says we are doing this today only to change plans at sunrise.

Get the agreement on paper; let him or her sign and make them understand that if they do not keep to their part, there'll be consequences. You know, there are people whom, in order to trust them, you need to help them by placing them in positions of discomfort. If your wife is a great administrator don't bother with administration, just give it to her. You don't outsource to a company that does not deliver; I'd rather do it myself. Seek to understand the person you are working with. It does not matter how long you have known the person. That you have been friends for 20 years doesn't mean you should continue to be friends after 20 years. If your brother cannot run the business, don't run the business on sentiment. Keep your brother in the house and place him on salary if you can; get someone who can run the business, you will make more money that way.

When you know your identity you will know your position. When you know your position you will be able to embrace your reality.

It's the truth, the average man will not want to hear this. Make sure you understand your partner. A couple came to me for marriage counseling and the woman looked at me and told me, pastor, I love him but I can no longer marry him. But I said madam it was love that made you marry him in the first place. Then she said that now she understands that love cannot even hold them. The word love there to them, only means affection; but love is beyond that. If you are working with a boss, take out the first 6 months to do a critical understudy of who you are working with. It will help you a great deal.

I used to work with a boss who cared less about salutations; all you needed to do to retain his smiles and friendship was to deliver. It didn't matter to him whether or not you greeted him; so long as you were delivering. Have an understanding of your partner understanding your partner, your partner does not like long sleeves and you went and bought a long-sleeved shirt; now you are angry that he has not worn it. No amount of persuasion exerted can make me wear a red suit . The blood of Jesus is enough. I don't care how much you bought it. It does not matter if it is G & G, Gucci or Armani. You bought it in Iceland or you bought it in heaven, it is none of my business. I don't like red suits. I don't like red shoes, and I don't like white shoes either. For what? the ground is dirty. Trying to make me wear these would be exerting energy in the wrong direction.

Have an understanding of what they like and don't like. If you buy me a colored shirt it might take me a very long time to wear it. If you buy a white shirt today, I will wear it in the evening. I've had a new white suit that someone bought me as

a gift. Oftentimes, I bring it out and take it to the dry cleaner, package and keep it back. As for when I'll wear it, I don't know. I am not Pastor Chris. Neither am I Benny Hinn, am I not Papa Oyedepo either. Is having a white suit bad? No, it does not just appeal to me.

One day I woke up and insisted it's time I wore the suit; that day my wife said I will not come to church because it would only take just about 40 minutes for me to get uncomfortable in it and send her to get me a change of cloth. Understand your partner.

Love is not the problem with so many relationships that have gone south; understanding is. You can love a person and still hate the person for not understanding you.

UNDERSTAND WHAT YOU ARE BUILDING

Understanding what you are building will save you time. Understand your assignment, know what you are supposed to be building. If you are a doctor, know that you are a doctor and you are going to be writing exams all your life. If you are a businessman, know that you are a business man and there'll be things to read and a few certifications to get. Know the certifications and start working towards getting them. Know what you are building. Don't be too archaic in a digital environment. As a civil engineer, know that there are certifications for engineers. The world is a village, you know you can get some of the certifications online. Sit down, read and get them. Some of them are not even expensive. Some of them are free courses that will give you an edge in your field of endeavor if you know what you are doing.

My people are destroyed for lack of knowledge. The children of this world are maximizing this things. Don't say grace did not work, grace works better when you have an edge. Know why it is not working. But pastor I will pray about it; good! When you are done praying, know why. Sometimes prayers should be for knowing why. Angels will not do for men what men should do themselves. If you don't tidy up your accounts in your establishments angels will not come to tidy up your account. Know what you are building.

As a musician, know your genre. The top gospel singers are known with their genres; when they come up, you already know if it's worship or praise. Have a brand; let people know you with one thing. I do not imply that you don't do every other thing but be known for one. If you don't know what you are building you will not know how to build it and you will not know who to associate with.

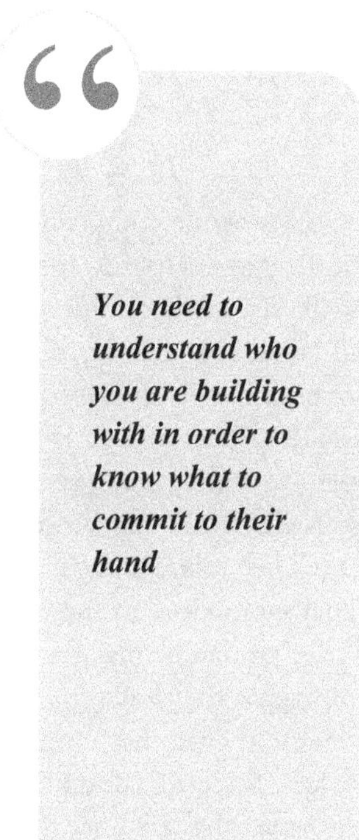

As a preacher, every preacher is not my friend. There are preachers I don't listen to; no matter how anointed they are. I don't listen to every preacher.

Apostle Paul said "these things I told you before I am saying again". Consistency becomes easy when you are know what you are doing.

There are people that will never come out of the deliverance ministry no matter how bad you talk about it. There is nothing you will do now to make me go back to the deliverance ministry; I will not. Why? Because I already know what I am building and how I am to build it. When you understand the assignment you will know who fits in and who does not. If you are a football lover, you will realize that where we are now in football is a very interesting place. It is where players are sold and players are bought. Every team has a philosophy and they buy players based on the philosophy of the team. I am a member of an international group belonging to the club I support. One day, someone recommended a player and immediately the response one of us gave to him was that though the player is a great player, yet he will not fit into the philosophy of the club. In my heart I knew that it was football that he was coming to play. Until you master the philosophy you will not be able to do that thing because psychologies have been built overtime. You'll agree with me that not every good singer can work with certain groups. Why? Because a pattern has been developed. Not every preacher can preach in my church and get the ears of the congregants to pay attention to him for up to 10mins before they sign out on him. Why will they sign out on him? A pattern has been put in place. Now if you don't understand this. You will carry the philosophy of the Ministry of Agriculture to work in the Ministry of Finance.

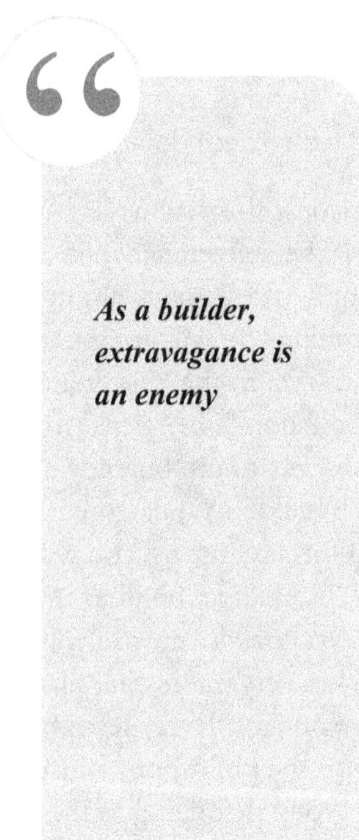

Sometime ago, someone complained to me about the presence of so many churches, while sin is still on the increase and I told him that more churches are coming. There are so many malaria drugs, yet malaria is still killing people. Now they are even mixing it, so malaria now has become very resistant. They mix it and call it Coartem. That's a mixture of three things that used to handle malaria independently; now they have become a threefold cord that cannot be easily broken. So more churches are going to come why? Because there are people that will never go to church if Deeper Christian Life centre was the only church in Nigeria. But there are also people that won't come to church if House on the Rock was the only church in Nigeria. God therefore, packages ministries based on the idiosyncrasies of men. So whichever one you fit into, get in and stay there. Have you never wondered at the choice of partner of someone before? You console yourself by telling yourself that it's their choice after all. All things great and small, tall and shot, slim and fat; the lord God made them all; he had our different choices in mind as he did.

Chapter eight

I—Impact

"I" stands for two things, one is impact, the other is inspiration.

Impact is the action of an object coming forcibly in contact with another object. When a car gets into an accident, people will always ask how much impact the car had. Now the truth about life is that life is all about impact. If you don't make impact people will not turn to your direction. Life is all about impact. Anybody you see on the news is making impact. If you don't make impact the news will not carry you. Now there are three types of impact.

What makes men stand out is impact. Don't fight a man that is outstanding; just make impact.

1) Positive impact.
2) Negative impact.
3) Nil impact.

The worst of these 3 impact types is Nil impact. People in this category are always there but never there. Jesus said be cold; that way we'll know you need help. Or be hot. But do not be neither hot nor cold, even he cannot manage you. He will spew you out of his mouth.

Looking at our world today we find different types of impact at play. Destitute nations of the earth are the way they are because of impact—negative ones at that. There are people that enter your life and your life starts to take a downward turn. They take you on a constant nose dive. There are others that enter your life and your life begins to appreciate. No matter what you are building please listen to me seek to make an impact in your generation. If you want to be a lawyer, make an impact. Whatever you are going to do, make sure that you make an impact. What makes men stand out is impact don't fight a man that is outstanding; just make impact. If you increase your impact you will automatically increase in influence. I have never seen an impactful person that is not influential.

When a child washes his hand well he will sit at the table with elders. If you are impactful nobody denies you. Make an impact with your service. Make an impact with your music. Make an impact with your product. You know some people make negative impact with their products. I have done business with people and I vowed never to recommend them to anyone because of impact—negative impact.

Make impact with your writing. Income follows impact; it's a principle. People pay you more when you have more impact. After getting a lot of headaches from mechanics, I finally found a trustworthy and well experienced one that I won't let go in a hurry. His charges are expensive but his services are impactful. Whatever you build, build with impact in mind.

To be impactful you will have to be honest; unless of course you intend for what you are building to die tomorrow. Unless of course you have a plan that will enable you escape seeing the people you see today again in 20 years; if not, then know for sure that they'll remind you of how you dealt with them today. Some of the people you are meeting now are only being introduced to you by God who knows you'll need them in 20 years' time but you just walk past them indifferently as though you'd never have any need for them in life. People have taken money from me and have remained poor. Beware of negative impact

Don't build to make money, build to make a name. If you make a name, you will make money.

Be sure it won't be the last time for you whenever you have the opportunity to make an impact.

A lot of Christians right now don't have a good name. Don't build to impress anybody, if there is anybody to be trusted in your company let that person be you. While I was growing up, my dad told me something; he said "see son when you tell the truth you won't try to remember what you said last time. You only try to remember what you said last time when you lied the last time". As a business person, you should know that customers don't forget. Sometimes people work for you and you know it's their last time; why? Negative impact. Be sure it won't be the last time for you whenever you have the opportunity to make an impact.

Commendation comes before recommendation. The news of a business transaction that didn't go well travels twenty times faster than that of a good business. People may never patronize your business because of a sad tale they heard someone tell about you.

Warren Buffet said get a good name, and after a while you won't need a complimentary card. The recommendations will be more than you can handle. No matter what you do, don't just be average, always leave an experience.

You need a lasting impact to build a lasting empire. The reason we have faith in God is because he is faithful. Be trustworthy; if you are worthy of trust, trust will come. If you are faithful, faith will come. We know God answers prayers, if he doesn't, I won't waste time to pray.

Don't win an argument and lose a relationship. People have lost people winning argument. Nobody has ever won a trophy for winning an argument. Be the fool but keep the relationship.

One day the person will wake up and respect you; he'll respect you because you let that go. A wise man had this to say about it: "saying I am sorry does not make you wrong, saying I am sorry only shows that you have more regard for the relationship than your ego".

Inspiration

But there is a spirit in man and the inspiration of the almighty giveth them understanding.

(Job 8:32)

People will forget how much you paid them but they won't forget how much impact you made in their lives. Impact generates influence. Impact and influence are directly proportional to each other. People gravitate to the place of impact.

A wise man said that the best revenge is to move on because most times trying to get revenge is distracting.

Don't change who you are to impress someone else.

There's a connection between bitterness and cancer; scientifically it's been proven that most bitter people die of cancer. The bible says bitterness is the rottenness of the bones. There's a connection between unforgiveness and the release of certain enzymes in your body that affects you negatively. When you accrue bitterness against someone, it's like drinking poison and expecting another to die (Nelson Mandela). Be who you are; people that will accept you for who you are in front; so don't change who you are so that when they come, they won't get confused.

Nobody has ever won a trophy for winning an argument. Be the fool but keep the relationship

Did you know that everyone you meet in life, you leave an impression? Whether consciously or unconsciously; deliberately or involuntarily, everyone you meet has something to remember you for. So be careful not to leave the wrong prints!

Make sure that you have something to be remembered for, wherever you go.

Think about this; if you had a month, a year or five years to leave where you are presently, have you done enough to be remembered for when you're gone?

A wise man said that you need to be continually inspired to walk the face of the earth; if not you will soon expire.

Matthew 5:14 says "you are the salt of the earth; if the salt loses its savor....." Now here's the statement that hit me; "it is good for nothing"...

It's still good but "for nothing"; it's good but not recommendable; good but cannot be promoted; good but cannot be married; the fact that he is good is not disputable just that he or she cannot be traded for anything.

He is good but economically he is on the minus scale; good but cannot be trusted to represent well; good but shouldn't be hung out with for doing so would be a waste of time. When the bible uses such statements, it gets me thinking. Now look at this; the bible says the only thing the salt is good for is "to be trodden underfoot by men". So sometimes when people treat us shabbily; it's not because they are rude. It's because of how you presented yourself. If you cannot add value, you are potentially an invalid. Your relationship with somebody is valid when you can add value. The day you stop adding value, you become a liability.

When you are not constantly inspired, you expire. Just like a shoe with an expired sole that wears out on its own. Some relationships are like that; they're already expired but we keep trying to work it out just like pumping an expired Tyre; it's time wastage because you'll always have need to visit a vulcanizer. All you need to do is change the Tyre. Whenever staying with the person makes you depressed instead of inspired— change the Tyre. Whenever they call you a spare, surprise them— dump them. They'll hate you but it's better than having to make a mess out of your life.

What does it mean to be inspired?

To be inspired means to be endued by the spirit with capacity to do something by supernatural or divine influence.

Job wrote this when the Holy Ghost was not yet living in man; at that time he still visited. So Job tried to differentiate between the spirit of man and the inspiration of the almighty which is the Holy Ghost because at that time, man was not yet joined with the Spirit of God.

Inspiration from on high is not true anymore for a New Testament believer. Every inspiration a born again Christian needs is not in heaven; it's within. Heaven lives within the Christian because of the Holy Ghost. The Holy Ghost is the active force of heaven that dwells in us; he is the thought-tank of God dwelling in man. He is the breath of God that made Adam a living soul. He is the incubator of God that incubated the earth before God spoke— living right inside us. So when Job was speaking, inspiration was coming from outside. It's no longer so; if you're born again, you just need to pick in. He is the believer's advantage. "There's a spirit in man"... That spirit was not the Holy Ghost, at the time Job was speaking, the spirit was dead. We see that it was impossible for that spirit to have understanding unless the inspiration of the Holy

Ghost was come upon it. So the activation of the spirit of man at that time depended upon the Holy Spirit.

We used to pray thus "take not your Holy Spirit from us....."

But the bible says that He that is joined with the Lord is one spirit. What this means is that when we get born again, our spirits are intertwined with the spirit of God. So he can't be taken away from us.

"If the spirit that raised Jesus from the dead abides in you.....

"Abide means he's no longer in heaven. It's like coming to church and saying "we enter your gates with thanksgiving and your courts with praise" where are you coming from? No more gates, you carry him! Residing in you is both the gate and the court so where are you entering.

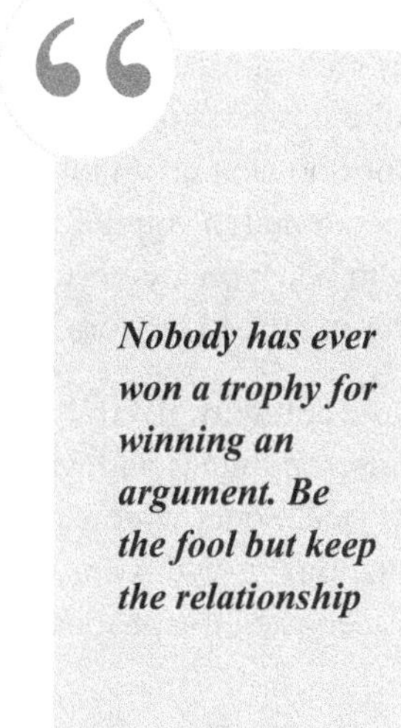

We sing the song "cast me not away, from your presence oh Lord; take not your holy spirit from me. Restore unto me... "What are you renewing? What has expired? You only renew expired licenses. You can't renew the Holy Ghost; how do you renew freshness? How can you? The Holy Ghost is the spirit of life; how can you renew life? When Job was saying this, he was still living in the outer court. Now we live in the Holy of holies.

Did you know that the mercy seat is not vacant right now? Jesus is seated on it. In the old covenant, the blood of bulls was sprinkled on the mercy seat. Jesus was the last sacrifice; every other sacrifice after him was and is illegal. Jesus is the sacrifice and he sits on the seat; now bidding us to come to the throne of grace that we may obtain mercy and grace for help in time of need. He's the one sitting there so no more sprinkling. He did it once and for all; as both the priest, the sacrifice and the seat.

So we don't pray Lord send us inspiration from heaven, it doesn't come as rain. "Now unto him that is able to do exceeding abundantly above all that we ask or think, according to the power that worketh in us, (Ephesians 3:20 KJV"). Often time we stop at the first part but see God says he won't do it from heaven; he'll do it from the potential in us. What's a potential? A potential is that which you have the ability to become but is yet to become. Now the Amplified Bible's rendition of that scripture tells us that the power is at work not in heaven but within us. Jesus speaking in the 17th chapter St Luke's gospel told us to stop looking for the kingdom without but to look for it within—"the kingdom of God is within you" he said. He wasn't speaking of heaven; no! Heaven is a place; the kingdom of heaven is an environment. Wherever the will of the king is actively enforced is his kingdom. So when people say they're carrying heaven inside them, they are not totally correct. You are not carrying heaven inside you; you're not carrying the streets of gold inside you; the 24 elders are not bowing down inside you; but there's a kingdom that becomes operational in you the moment the Holy Ghost comes in to reside in you; you are brought under the influence and ruler-ship of the power of the kingdom.

"There is a spirit in man; the inspiration of the almighty giveth him understanding"... Both the spirit and the understanding is with you! The spirit and the understanding are actually one. So its safer and better to put it this way; the spirit of understanding is with you, within you and functional in you. If it's not seen then the problem is with you; not God.

To be inspired or have inspiration is to be filled with exalted influence. Inspiration is the God factor manifested in man; it means to infuse into the mind or to communicate to human spirit—definite solutions by the influence of the supernatural. It means to be breathed into. Consider Genesis 2; God created man and man was just there until he breathed into man, then man became a living "nephesh" (Hebrew rendition of the word translated soul). A living soul, mind, emotion; a living psyche, a living thought. It's the Holy Ghost that quickens the soul.

"Without inspiration, there is no innovation"

Don't ever build without your advantage—the Holy Ghost. Without inspiration, there is no innovation. Those times in your walk as a builder (whether as a career person or as a business person) when there's no solution anywhere near, what do you do then? You go "in". We don't live outside in; we live inside out. You go in and bring it out. The bible says that counsel in the heart of a man is like deep waters but a man of understanding will draw it out

. Right inside your spirit is seated, every solution you need but there are dimensions to fetchers. There are fetchers that can never get deep down enough to the point where your need is. Understanding is the fetcher; there are dimensions to understanding. When you tell a child that's in Nursery to add A to A or 6a to a, he'll tell you it cannot work. That's a level of understanding; as he advances he steps up to the place he realizes that such thing as a+a exists with equations. At the nursery level, he's only taught the simple arithmetic of adding 1 to 1 to get 2. You even use the abacus to help him understand numbers; but then a time comes when he grows into the level of understanding where he's able to solve 6ab+6ab-2c+2c. Some people are on that level of understanding while others are on the second; but some others have also gotten to the point of solving $yx(a-b)^2/ xy$; this is whole new level of understanding. The person on this 3rd level, understands all three levels; the person on level 2 doesn't understand level 3 but he understands level 1; and the person on the first level only understands that level but doesn't understand the other two.

Those whom God has brought to that third level spiritually easily connect and pick up spiritual frequencies. The true and amazing thing about growing into these dimensions is that there's no timeline attached to it; you can grow at the speed of light because you don't need to travel to call. What you need is there in you; now this is deep. This is where all inventions come from. Your dreams are a function of your business; if you frequently watch horror movies, you'll have horrible dream. Because it's a function of what you put seated in your subconscious. That's why retreats are very important. A retreat is not going to camp for a special time of prayer. A retreat is you taking out time to review your progress and effectively initiate improvement plans. Even during your prayer time; prayer time is not necessarily a time to talk. Prayer is not a monologue; it's a dialogue. Usually we go in to the place of prayer and murmur, talk, complain, wail, mourn, nag; and just walk away without getting out information. Information is there but we're often in too much hurry to get any out of the place of prayer. They told you it's a time to get to talk to God; no! It's a time to talk with God; God also wants to talk to us. His spirit within us is a speaking spirit; he always wants to tell us what to do. This is why some people have to fall sick before they can hear God; that's when they become calm enough to worship and look into scriptures. For some people, God has to let the devil arrange trouble just to slow us down because they're often in a hurry.

This is what makes you stand out from everyone else; except born again Christians like you too. If you can hear God well, you won't always go to your pastor to ask questions because God doesn't always have to go through your pastor to get to you; he can talk to you. You're going to the man of God will be for confirmation. He becomes a second witness.

As you build, you'll get to a place where you get stuck; without inspiration you can't move any further. That's where people start consulting soothsayers; and start going to prayer houses. You are looking for a wife and you're confused; all you need to search. There's a well within you; it's a well of information. The bible calls it the wisdom for witty inventions. And it's not a onetime thing. In your building journey, matters will arise; will you always know what to do? Jesus, when he was here on earth had about five thousand men (minus women and children; estimated to be about fifteen thousand) to feed one time after he had spoken for three days so he called Phillip to get food. You need sufficient food to feed about twenty thousand people, lest you have yourself a stampede. If that happened be sure you'll have someone die and if anyone died there, the Jews would have had something to say against him because they had eyes on him all that time. Know this; as you build, people will keep eyes on you for loopholes. Jesus could confidently say that they found nothing on him; will you be able to say the same?

What happened was that those people were enraptured into the realm (a consciousness) of God's sweet word which can substitute every necessity in life including food; God's word has that sustaining ability too. At the time Jesus spoke to Philip, they we're no longer suspended under that consciousness. The bible says that Jesus knew what to do; now that's my point—inspiration. A king had a dream, woke up, and called his magicians to tell him his dream and the interpretation. The magicians told him to tell them the dream and they'd tell him the interpretation but he said no. Now who does that? It's like giving a target of #700 million to a banker that doesn't know anybody. So they told him that what he was asking was above the level of men and could only be found with the gods. When some things come up in your organization and everybody is saying it cannot be done, don't open your mouth. Because it cannot be found on the level of men; it's always amongst the gods and the last time I checked, the bible says "ye are gods"... Now what thrills me about this whole story is the confidence in Daniel's response; that could only come from knowledge. So the question is, what did Daniel know to answer with such boldness for three days to be given to him? As a Christian you will not always know what to do but know that there's something you carry that makes you know what to do once you kick into it—that is a dimension. As a Christian you have been forbidden from saying it cannot be done. Lying in your inside, is the impossibility specialist. If you can think possibility, then leave the rest to him; he knows how to fix it.

I realized that no one gives you a bill for dreaming. There are two things that makes people go far in life; dreams and talks. Nobody bills you for doing these two. God says "You shall have whatsoever you say"; that's a blank check. God so designed it that we do not pay to talk; except of course when you want to do it through a medium such as a mobile phone, then your network provider charges you for talk time. As for talking, it is always said that talking is cheap. Nobody bills you for dreaming, it's always "as far as your eyes can see". Don't get envious when someone tells you their dream; close your eyes and dream too. These are two things God has given us to move our lives forward; we don't get to pay to use them yet we don't even use them. What did Daniel know? Daniel knew that he had access to a dimension; a dimension deeper than Joseph's; a dimension deeper than interpreting dreams and cracking codes; a dimension where you enter into someone's mind and dig out the dream he dreamt the previous night; even when the man that dreamed the dream forgot his dream. Inspiration! That's where innovations such as iOS, Androids and smart phones are coming from. Soon people will write in air.

Oftentimes we build boundaries where God has left limitless but Daniel knew what he had. He confidently asked for three days. There are matters that do not give you time for testing out different water; in such cases, you need inspiration. There's a spirit in man, and lying in the new creation man is the inspiration of the almighty. You cannot build anything that will last beyond time if the inspiration doesn't come from him that lives outside time. If you want to do things like every other person, you'll be in the competition but when you do things above the normal, you will be the competition; because he that is from above, is above all. Things will get hooked up— do you know what button to press? Business will get stuck— do you know what button to press? When people walk up to you at your work place saying that you're being a threat to them and that they'd deal with you; do you know what to do? You wake up at midnight to a strange figure at your door and turning back from it would mean trouble; standing face to face with it—do you know what to do? You submit a proposal for a contract and someone threatens you to withdraw or be damned—do you know what to do? When you are tempted and threatened to do things that are against your faith—do you know what to do? One of the things I love hearing is that someone is a force to contend with—a negative force; he'll sleep and chase himself in his dreams.

Inspiration puts you above the pack. It is mostly triggered by passion for what you're building. Passion opens up the portals for inspiration. Inspiration pays in mind blowing percentages. It makes you do the ordinary in an extraordinary way. Inspired people are not normal, they're people that live above the normal. In today's world where everything is getting scientific, we need to become more spiritual. Inspiration brings you to realms where solutions emerge by themselves.

No matter what you do, keep your inspiration lines open.

I realized that life has a way of discarding and abandoning emptied containers or people. Naturally things and people flow in the direction of the supply-source of their wants and needs.

This world is a battleground. Paul said in 2 Tim 4:7-8 that "he had fought a good fight; he had finished his course and kept the faith". Do you know that to finish your course and to keep the faith is a fight? Do you know what to do to contend with the prophecy that has gone ahead of you and make sure it comes to pass?

Take out a moment and say this prayer; say "Lord may I always be in a position to know always, what to do".

Jesus had about twenty five thousand people to feed, yet he knew what to do. You'd say but "he's Jesus" but looking at Jesus, you'd find out that he grew in his manifestations. He started by turning water to wine to the point where he spoke to the wind and the waves and they calmed down; he grew to the point where he walked on water. He didn't just become God all at once; he grew into that nature because he was a man too; God doesn't grow, men do! He grew in manifestations. Don't say I can't do it; what you should be doing at your level now, can you do it? God told you that you have a gift of healing; what are you doing now at your level? You should start with a headache; when you heal a headache then you can proceed onto stomach aches; before you know it, you're handling incurable diseases; it's growth. God has given to every one of us a measure of faith; but it's like muscles. If you don't go the gym, your muscles won't grow; your muscles grow by reason of use. That's what happens when we hear God; you hear him, you knew he was the one but you silenced the voice; you heard him again and you silenced him. What happens is you stop hearing. But when you hear and do what he says, overtime his voice becomes clearer. Its comes hazy at first but as you hear and do what he says, it becomes clear; you don't have clarity of God's voice; you grow into it.

Inspiration drops every day; do you write it down when it comes? Do you keep it safe? What will give you an edge in your career, business and academics is inspiration. It feels good to know what's coming out for an exam before actually seeing the script.

May God show you what next to do in Jesus' name, amen.

I won't be where I am today if I hadn't heard God clearly. I had just concluded my service year with the ambition go to into the corporate world when God told me to leave the city where I was and come back to South Eastern Nigeria and help my senior pastor at House On The Rock church, Enugu State. I asked God how my senior pastor could be helped by me; and he said "move". I lost a relationship because of that but I'm happy I did. I had my plans to become perhaps an associate professor of Geology by now but God said drop those ambitions of yours and go back. When I went to lament to the pastor that I was under then, he said "son everyone that God calls, leaves something behind". In the end, I followed because I heard. Now my classmates call me and seek counsel from me, my bosses in the city of Jos where I left, call me for prayers and after these they appreciate me with offerings; now I'm glad I heard and followed. This book is a possibility today because I heard.

Bishop David Oyedepo of Living Faith Church worldwide said when they got to the large bush area that is presently the site of their headquarters, his pastors asked him what they had come there to do. He said the moment they stepped into the land, he heard God say "this is the place"; now looking at Winner's Chapel Headquarters today, is that not the place? Don't waste your time driving with an expired tire; don't spend time trying to move a car that has refused to move. Inspiration will tell you when the time of a thing has finished.

In August 2015, God told me to take a job; I told my wife and she said "get a job you say? I thought you said you were going to be doing ministry? I told her that God said so; and that he said I'd be doing the job for one year. She said "I have no doubts because it has always been God that spoke every time you said he did". Not up to three days later, a senior friend came to my house to tell me about a managerial job opening in his company; and that I should announce the vacancy in church based on trust that the church would produce the most qualified hand for the job. We finished talking and he left the house, he had already driven out and I was already in the house when I heard: "that's the job I was telling you about". Immediately I called my friend back and told him I will do the job and he was surprised. I went for the interview and they said I didn't have the experience for the job; I had never done a pharmaceutical job before so I left. A week later, they called me and told me that there was another managerial job—a higher one at that; this one covered the whole nation. I accepted the offer, went to my pastor to get his blessings only to get there and he refused to release me. So I wrote back a letter of declination to the company and went back to the church office. I was supposed to resume at the job in September but by December that year, I met their head of sales; he said to me "pastor you don't want to come take your job? " Surprised, I asked him which job? He said the CEO said the job was mine and that if after December I didn't show up to accept it, then they'd give it to another. In three months according to him, more than forty people had come for the job. This job had an official car, petrol allowance, and so many other allowances.

I took the job. The interesting thing is that when I got to the place, the MD on seeing me asked "are you now ready to take the job?" I said yes and he said "okay"; called on the secretary to get my files and after that he asked me to write "I accept" and sign it on the same declination letter. I started the third of January and by June that year, God said time up! That was on my birthday; I asked but "Lord you said one year?" Two weeks later my pastor showed up and told me to get ready for a pastoral appointment in the city where I now pastor. I went back to my CEO and told him "sir remember that when I took the job, I told you I am a priest and may be needed anytime; I may be leaving here anytime soon so we need someone who can take over from me on standby ". He said it's okay that when it's time, I could leave. By September that year, I was scheduled to meet with The Metropolitan Head of my church and was told to prepare to come over to Lagos anytime I was called for a refresher course of about six months. I went back and told my boss, "see I don't know when they'd call me but I'm leaving soon". By December 22nd I got the email, printed it out and took it to my boss. He said "okay when we resume in January, you can resign". Remember I resumed with them on the fourth (4th) of January. Now here's the amazing thing, I resigned from the job on the 3rd of January, not an extra day was added to the one year.

When I met my wife, I was already tired of relationships but God told me that what I was looking for was around me; today the rest is history.

Inspiration sometimes says what you're not saying; what it shows you sometimes may not look like the picture you want to see. But it doesn't need to look like it to be it. You need to listen well to hear well; as a lady God shows you who you're to marry and he's poor so you argue; my dear listen well. The rich man you want may be touching his last wealth and the poor guy you see may be a bundle of wealth in the making; listen well. So you don't use physical eyes and walk into what you're walking out from. The rich guy you're crushing on now, may be driving his last range rover. When my wife and I got married, I only had a house, a car and #970 in my account. The car was there because I vowed never to sell my things; the # 970 was there because I couldn't withdraw #500. She married me nonetheless and today we are still eating the #970, feeding many from it and will still feed more, will still do so much more than we're already doing.

Listen to God! This is the edge we have. There's a spirit in man—you have it; the inspiration of God—you have it. You read the bible, pray in tongues yet your eyes still deceive you. You've been led to do a business and you're checking "how many people are doing it?" Well no one needs to do the business for you to start. God may be trying to use you to break grounds. Habakkuk said "I'll stand upon my watch, to see what he'll say to me.... "Inspiration! "And what I will answer when I am reproved". Know for sure that life will reprove you but it is what you get from him that you'll answer life. It's good to be bold, it's wonderful to have understanding, it's great to make impact but if you're not inspired always, very soon the impact will fade. People that are always on the news are people that always do new things. If you don't constantly do new things, you cannot be on the news. Always give life something to chew by the inspiration you get from him.

As long as you're hearing God men will hear you. You need to hear God to be on the frontline in whatever area it is you're trying to build something. You cannot be inspired and expire; no way! Because that which makes life, life, works in you. Will what you're building get stuck sometimes? Yes! Will you run out of idea sometimes? Yes you will! But there is a spirit in man; the inspiration of the almighty gives him understanding.

Chapter nine

Most times, God packages our help in unlikely containers

L-everage L-eadership

Under the letter L, we'll be considering two factors namely Leverage and Leadership.

Leverage is by extension, any influence which is used to gain an advantage. Take for instance the well-known Toyota Car company. They do not produce brake pads, shaft; they don't produce tires; some parts of the engine too. One time Honda wanted to work with Toyota but Toyota refused. Surprisingly, that which Toyota pointed out is still Honda's problem today. When Toyota wanted to start out, he met with Honda and told Honda to make shafts. Honda did and brought the shafts to Toyota. On examination, Toyota rejected the shaft due to its incompetence. Honda got offended and started making his own cars; decades later, up till present day, Honda's shafts are still the problem with their cars. As you grow, whichever problem you fail to handle promptly is a ward problem when it exposes you. As you go higher it becomes a local government problem; further it becomes a district problem. At a point, it becomes a global problem if not attended to.

Leverage is not parasitic in nature. A parasitic relationship is one that involves two people, namely: a host and the parasite. Do not kill yourself and to impress others. The only person worthy such thing as of you displeasing yourself to please is God.

Matthew 17:24-27 it was not right for Jesus to pay tithe but lest he offended the people, he did. Jesus needed to pay tax but he wasn't a fisherman, the money he wanted to use to pay the tax was in a fish's mouth so he leveraged on his relationship with Peter. When you need to paint, you get a painter, if a carpentry job, you leverage on a carpenter. Leverage on your relationship with a professional to get a professional need met. Leverage on the person that has what you don't have. One of my mentors told me this: "Lend your company to people so that they can do with your company what you cannot do with your company".

Luke 5:1-6 Always take note of this in your relationships. The first text shows that Jesus needed Peter, the second text showed how Peter needed Jesus.

Don't be too proud to ask for help. I can never do an electrical job in my church no matter how I'm led but I'll let the electrician know that there's something in me he needs to get the wires wired; that's leverage. Often Christians think that a fellow Christian should always do their jobs for them free and they end up paying the unbeliever hugely; foolishness at its peak.

Don't be too proud to ask for help. The truth is that the face that makes money doesn't get ashamed. David saw Goliath and knowing that he was going to be meat for the birds, he asked "what will be given to the man that brings his head down". The disciples followed Jesus and after a while, Peter asked "What shall be given to us who has left everything to follow you". God taught us leverage, he couldn't come down to carry Jesus as pregnancy and deliver him as a woman, so he used Mary. Mary became the most popular woman on earth through that and the Catholic Church has become the richest single organization on earth through Mary.

Leverage on the people around you. Allow yourself to be used to get what you want. Only proud people are unusable. No business on the earth can flourish by being by and for one person only.

Peter needed Jesus to get cash, Jesus needed Peter's skill.

As a business person leverage on integrity. Build alliances. When I was coming to the city where I currently pastor, I asked God to give me a family for a church. So that I can push the things that pass by me to the church family. In my church I teach leverage and we practice it. We practice partnership and corporation such that almost every need is met in and by the house because we have people in almost every field of life.

It is important to let people know what you do and know what people do; the day will come when you will have need for each other. What we call connection is simply people knowing each other and what each one does. Angels don't build. I have never read nor seen where it is written in the scriptures that angels build. No! God gave that mandate to man.

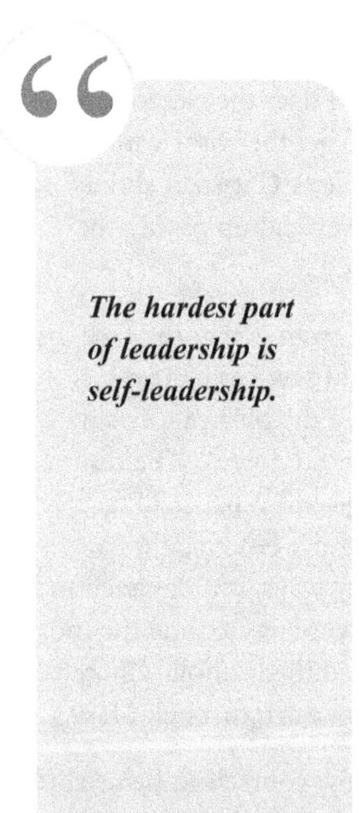

There is this innate ability in man that makes him repel a thing when it doesn't look like him. People have the tendency to antagonize something that is not like them. But most times God packages our helps in containers that are unlike us. God sends us people to help us with things we cannot do. One of the things a woman helps a man do is give birth. Trans gendering cannot solve this. When God said he'd send suitable help to man, he factored in pregnancy and mensuration. Imagine there were no women; men would have to do it all. We'd become bisexuals, hermaphrodites. We'd literally have to impregnate ourselves, carry the pregnancy and deliver it. That would have been crazy right? When God wants to send us help, he doesn't send us helps that look like us. He sends us helps that differ from us but is still headed the same direction as us. So a nut meets a bolt and if the nut says because the bolt doesn't look like me, I will not work with it, then it will be useless. A nut that isn't locked is a useless nut. It takes a bolt to lock a nut.

So what the nut does is it leverages on what the bolt has which it doesn't and purpose is accomplished.

The man that insists on being both the author and finisher of what he's building, is actually building nothing. Because no matter how small what you're building is, you need people. When God wants to discipline a man with a wicked thing, he leverages on a naturally wicked person. Remember when he asked David who he preferred to be disciplined by; he (God) or his (David's) enemies? David knew that his enemies had been waiting for him to fall into their trap so he begged the Lord to let it be at his hands that he'd suffer chastisement. Because he (God) is a merciful and forgiving God.

According to the scriptures, God would naturally let Israel fall into the hands of Assyria whenever he wanted to deal with him because the Assyrians were naturally wicked. When he wanted to hide the Hebrew spies, he used Rehab—a professional at hiding things. She hid not one spy, but two. Jews don't travel light, they go on their journeys with everything they'd need because they cannot share personal things with gentiles, such as those of Jericho; they consider it defilement. Those spies must have traveled heavily packed with everything they needed for their journey. Yet Rehab was able to hide them neatly; such that no traces of their presence was found. Note also that it was soldiers who interrogated and searched Rehab's house—military intelligence.

Leverage will save you a lot of stress and help you cut building cost. For car owners, if you are careful enough to observe, you'll find that your car brand doesn't make everything with which they make cars—it's called leverage.

Leverage on the people around you and be leverage worthy. That's why banks do what we call outsourcing services. They do so because they're too busy to do everything for themselves. People go to dry-clean their clothes at the dry cleaner's because they're too busy to do so for them not because they are rich. It's foolishness to take your clothes to a drycleaner when you have both time and the resources to do it yourself. That's a waste of useful money. Don't try to be what you're not or who you are yet to become. Allow yourself to get there, things will naturally start to react by themselves when you do.

Leadership

It is not possible to build anything without leadership. Leadership is the act of influencing others or serving others with the interest of helping them achieve their purpose and so that you can also achieve your purpose through them.

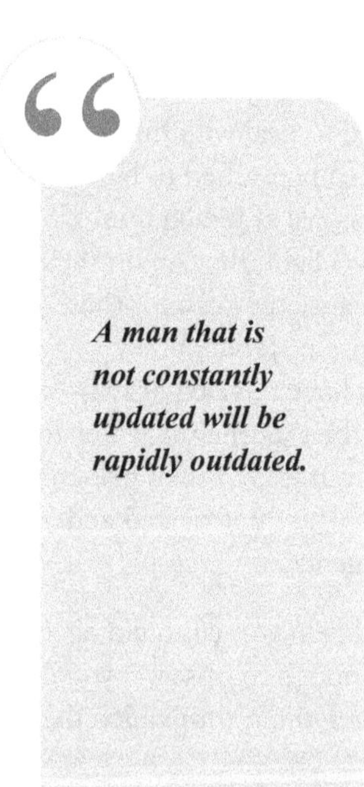

For where there's existence, wherever there's organization, leadership must be in place. Where there's no hierarchy, there's bound to be anarchy and nothing can be built in anarchy. Whether it's a ministry you're building, a career, a business, a Christian life, a church, family and what have you; leadership must be in place.

Leadership cannot happen if the leader has not yet first learnt to lead him or herself. The hardest part of leadership is self-leadership. This is because it entails enforcing on yourself the discipline that will enable you to become that which you aim to be, that which you've decided to be and that which you've set as a goal to be.

The great leadership consultant John Maxwell is an authority in this area, his texts are highly recommended materials on this topic.

Leadership is possible only by influence. A person who wants to really lead must be first a person of influence.

If leadership is about influence than the first person to lead is yourself. One who cannot lead himself cannot effectively lead others. A leader is not to oppress or overpower others by his authority, no! He is meant to lead and that by influence.

THE PRINCIPLES OF EFFECTIVE LEADERSHIP

- LOVE

Love is very central to human life. It's a basic psychological need of man; one of the highest. You cannot lead a people you don't love.

You end up ruling over the people you don't love and not leading. You end up being a bully instead when you don't love the people you claim to lead. You have to be concerned about their wellbeing. Before going after people's hands, go first for their hearts. Love people

People naturally want to be led by those who love them.

In our generation, we tend to love things and use people instead of the other way…

People respond to love and that response is submission and loyalty. When you genuinely and willingly love people, they will willingly follow you; that's how they respond to your love.

- MODESTY

To be able to lead a people successfully, you need to be modest. Do not be the I-know-it-all leader. Do not force people into submission. Remember that leadership is all about influence. Pride bible says, goeth before destruction, and a haughty spirit before a fall. Better it is to be of a humble spirit with the lowly, than to divide the spoil with the proud (Proverbs 16:17-18). People tend to submit more when they know that you're an easy going person.

Indeed sometimes they tend to take you for granted but being bossy doesn't make it better. Let the people following you know that you're human too. It doesn't reduce their respect for you. Do not be proud.

The bible says that God gives grace to the humble; that is to say that the grace for leadership comes upon the humble too. Humility is key to great leadership. Pride has never and will never pay any sensible wage. The way to attract grace and followership is by being humble. Don't stay up and expect your people to meet you at your level, come down to their level and lead them up. About Jesus, the bible says that he's not the kind of priest who is not touched with the feelings of our infirmities. As a leader, be touched with the feelings of the infirmities or weaknesses of the people that are following you. This is one of the greatest attributes of a good leader.

- SELF-DEVELOPMENT

You must pay attention to self-development. Jesus, our perfect example, would constantly slip away into the mountains to develop himself. Be keen about self-development. If you don't develop yourself, the people you're leading will soon catch up with you and get ahead of you. Add to what you know and have. Keep learning, constantly be about improvement and update. What are the things you need to know or have to achieve your desired goals? Go for it! Attend seminars and conferences. Go for symposiums; go get an extra certification in your area of interest. No knowledge is a waste. A man that is not constantly updated is rapidly outdated. Pay attention to self-development. Develop yourself so much that you're always ahead. To be the head, you have to be ahead. Pay attention to the things that your mentors read. If you fail to do so, the intellectually-curious ones among your followers will overtake you. Yes! Those who are on the quest for knowledge will always want to know what you know and how you know what you know. You'll be doing yourself good by constantly setting the pace.

- MOTIVATION

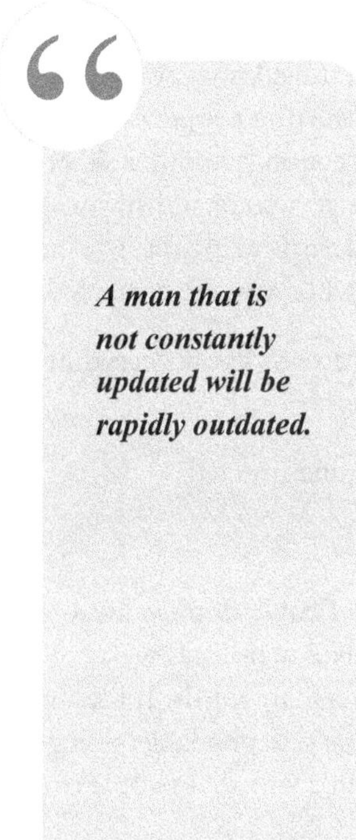

A leader has to be internally motivated. You have to motivate yourself beyond any reasonable doubt. Don't depend on external motivations for what God has called you to build. Sometimes we find the people we seek motivations from, also in need of motivation. It is necessary to remain the most reliable source of your own motivation. Motivate yourself from within—you carry so much power in there. It takes self-motivation to enable a person to motivate others, know the things that stir you and pay attention to them. The things that trigger you and make you want to do things. Know them and stay with them. Life has up times and down times. In the down times of life, self-motivation is inestimably important. Go for both internal and external motivation. It pays to always have someone around you whose job is not to tell you a lie but to motivate you.

Also motivate the people you lead. Don't just be the type that sees just the faults. Give them reasons to follow you. Make it impossible for them to leave you; so much so that when they do, they'll look for ways to come back. Make them believe in themselves. Pay attention to their motivation. People will follow a man that talks well to them; a man that tells them how big they can become, how far they can go even when they mess up.

HAVE THE NERVE TO CORRECT.

Correction is important in building. Leaders know how to correct the people they lead and that correctly. Be intentional. That's why you're a leader. When they go wrong, you must know how to correct. Correction is very important. Correcting people is one side of it; being humble enough to accept correction is another side of it. Do not be the leader that allows things go wrong and stay wrong because they're the ones at fault. You will earn the people's respect when you accept and react the right way when you are corrected.

Being humble enough to accept that you do not know everything is wisdom.

As a leader, make sure that no error goes uncorrected.

- **INTEGRITY**

Good leaders value and practice integrity. People don't value a person who lacks integrity. Integrity involves actions as well as words. Sometimes it involves more actions than words. It involves practicing what you say. Being consistent and dependable; doing what you say you will do and living in such a way that people trust you.

Righteous lips are the delight of kings and they love him who speak right ***(Prov 16:13)***

Integrity is integral in building anything formidable.

Any leader who lacks integrity is a time waster. Without integrity reasonable people will have nothing to do with you. The bible says "let our yes be yes and let your no be no". Most times we water down our leadership qualities because of lack of integrity.

Let your life reflect integrity and soon you will have people following you on the basis of trust.

- **BE APPRECIATIVE**

Be in the habit of thankfulness and gratitude at all times. Always find a way to appreciate the people that follow you. It gives them a sense of value; this is another great psychological need of man. The need to feel valued. When you do this, people become faithful to you and your course natural as a way of responding to your kindness. This is a small thing really but it does a lot. Never let saying "thank you" be a big task to you. Make it a habit.

Love people, be modest, correct and be corrigible and finally, be thankful. These simple quotients make for a successful and effective leadership.

Chapter ten

D-Determination

The grass is greener where it is watered. If you water your grass, it will be green

Daniel 1:8 "But Daniel determined in his heart that he would not defile himself by [eating his portion of] the king's rich and dainty food or by [drinking] the wine which he drank; therefore he requested of the chief of the eunuchs that he might [be allowed] not to defile himself.

No one has ever built anything successfully without having determined to do so. One of the greatest nations on earth is the determine-nation.

Determination is the mental quality of having firm or fixed intention to reach a concluded end or achieve a desired goal. The bible speaking in the book of James, tells us that a man that's tossed to and fro, a man that wavers should not think he'd receive anything from God. One of the greatest criterions of great builders is that they are determined. Some-times so determined that you'll think they're proud. David said his face was set as a flint. We would not have salvation if Jesus was not determined. He said in John 9:4 "I must work the works of him that sent me while it is day........... " Every man that is building knows that if he isn't determined, time can choke him. At age 30, you're already behind time. If you're in a third world country like Nigeria, you're at disadvantage. For someone born here, you need to be extra determined. If you want to build anything especially in this part of the world, then know that you must be determined. There are so many things around us bent on making sure we don't succeed.

I was speaking with a Lebanese living in Ghana, sometime ago and he said to me: "for being an African, you're already disadvantaged. They'll look first at a light-colored person, no matter where he is from before they'll look at you; so you have to prove yourself". That's why when I see young people who only know how to chat with their smart phones, I see someone praying against the weapons of darkness and he is that weapon he's praying against. There's so much one can do online. You can become almost anything with Google these days. I am more informed with Google than I am with books because some of the information I have in books are so outdated that they cannot be relied upon. The world is advancing at a very fast rate and everything around you is built to keep you down, you have to determine and tell yourself, it's not true. Our education systems is so far behind in innovation and global intelligence. You find people studying computer science and engineering in higher institutions here still being taught quad-rants, still being taught Q-basic. What are they doing with those in 2021 when some of the phones we use are being developed by 14year olds? Everything around, wants to make sure that you're on the floor.

Let me say this "if you're still thinking about getting your kids to study medicine and law, you're still far behind time". The children of kings don't study medicine and Law. How many political heads do you know whose children study medicine and law? Few I believe! They get their kids to study Political science, Philosophy, Psychology, (Human Psychology, now they've even entered into Robotic Psychology). I hold nothing against formal education but these days BSC don't do much anymore. Even multinational companies now accept people with normal certificate courses. You'll be shocked at what on-line certificate courses can do for you. The world has become a global village. If your thinking is still within the range of your local surrounding, then my friend you're still primitive. Like I earlier said, the place we call destiny is not far; it's the places we branch off to before getting there that makes it look far. Know dear friend that you do not have time. Building is like driving a bus. If you're going to check on every Dick and Tom you meet on the way then you surely are in for a long ride. But if you focus and determine to reach your destination on time, you will. When someone gets down, replace him quickly and get going; you don't have time. You graduated five years ago and you told yourself that you were going to get a masters; now its five years and you're still the same Bsc holder. You don't even know its five years already. You said you were going to write that book, but its six years already, what happened? Distractions! You said you were going to settle down but you kept checking out every guy and every girl to know if they were the right ones. Every time a new guy shows up, your relationship starts having issues because you'd like to try out the new guy to see if he's the one. Now it's already 13 years and you're still waiting. You need to sit down and remind yourself of your age. Doing this will correct some stupid thinking in some people. Most times youthful exuberance confuses us so that we forget that we're ageing. You find a young man and ask him his age, then he tells you he's "only" 32; only! Perhaps the day you start to de-fine 32 as 8 years down from 40, maybe then your thinking will be correct-ed. Some people go to school to study a course of six years simply because their parents want them to. They go ahead to waste six full years of their lives living their parent's lives—a borrowed life.

> *the formula for failure is "trying to make everybody happy"*

"Daniel determined in his heart that he would not defile himself....." Please know that when it comes to determination, you are alone. There are no general convictions with determination. Whatever you have set for yourself as a goal, you have to lock your heart to achieve it. The day I found out that I'd be a pastor, I locked my heart; till today, I'm still get-ting offers. If I hadn't done so, I'd still be wavering by now. The grass is never greener on the other side; the grass is greener where it is watered. If you water your grass, it will be green.

That time you finally make up your mind to do business, that's when job offers may troll you—distraction. That time you finally decide to marry, that's when the flashiest girls will start coming around you—distraction. The power of the laser is the power of focus. If you're not focused, you will not be able to cut anything in life. Any man that is not determined will be left behind by life. There are so many reasons to not do what you want to do. Discouragements will come. Worse still, they may come from the very people you look up to for encouragement; but be determined. Are you sure about it? Yes! Have you prayed about it? Yes! Do you have peace with it? Yes too! But know this; a time will come when those whose words are al-ways steady will come to you with divergent news. When they do, remember that your destiny is your destiny; your vision is your vision. Whether or not you'll be deceived, is your choice, your decision. The outcome of your life is a product of your choices. Weaklings don't build anything. If you let other people influence your choices, remember that in the end, the outcome will be yours and fully yours to bear or enjoy. Be intentional about your decisions. Find out what others know and do what they do so long as it's not against your faith. Be wise as the serpent. I am in ministry because I am called. Any day

God shows up and says the call has expired (though there's no such thing) I'll be in the next city by sundown. I'm determined because I am called.

Be determined to build what you're building, your payday will come. Don't follow trends. Be the brand and be determined to build it. Let people know you for what you're building, when a need arises that is in your area of specialization, they will not hesitate to call you. When you are determined, you won't know when years will go by. Your credibility is determined by your longevity.

As you build, challenges will come, troubles may arise, and people and circumstances will fight you. Tobias' and Sambalats will arise but be determined. Fix your gaze on your mark, fix your gaze on your price. Don't look at the prevailing circumstances. Put your focus on that which you build. The bible speaking of Jesus in Hebrews 12:2, says looking unto Jesus the author and finisher of our faith. Who for the joy that was set before him, endured the cross." Jesus was determined. When you are determined, you cannot say how much and how far you can go. That single determination and purposing which Daniel did, made him relevant to four kings. Build what you're building to be the paradigm of excellence, such that when people want to talk about it, they talk about it as the best. If you're determined, you'll build a legacy. Undetermined minds can't build legacies.

A determined person may fall, but don't write him off be-cause he'll soon be back. Little wonder Micah told us in Micah 7:8 saying, "rejoice not over me my enemy; for when I fall, I shall rise. Though I sit in darkness, the Lord will be my light." Though the righteous fall seven times, he will rise again. Life will knock you down but whether life will knock you out is your decision to make. For as long as you keep coming back to the ring, you're not knocked out. Be determined. You dropped out of school? Go back! The business failed? Start again! They sacked you from your job? Write another proposal. Les Brown wanted to be a DJ but they wouldn't take him. He kept going back but still they wouldn't oblige. One day he was so drunk and nothing was happening in the radio station. The director called him and asked "Les what are you doing there?" He said "I'm working" the director said "but there's nothing happening there; okay you know what? Do this and that and that and don't do anything else". That was the long awaited opportunity he had been anticipating. He went in there, picked up the microphone and never came down again. As a sales person, they'll say you can't get one "Yes" until you've had five "Nos". You can't do it? Who said so? Nobody's opinion matters until you've chosen to let it matter. You can do it if you learn it! If dogs can learn then my friend you have no excuse; be determined! They said it cannot be done and you believed? Now life is hard because you lived what you believed. Your outcome is a function of your beliefs too. Where is your heart? Put your hand there. The bible says that he that puts his hands on the plough and not even removes it but look backs, is not worthy.

Now I put the question to you dear reader. Are you deter-mined enough to take what you want out of life? Life gives you nothing on a platter. Whatever you want, you have to be determined enough to take it. What do you want to have? Be determined; go after it and it will be yours.

- **DEVOTION**

Life is spiritual. Life is more than what we see, touch, feel and hear. Another word for devotion is commitment. Devotion however goes beyond commitment because commitment can be in part but devotion goes a long way, right into worship and the committing of one's entire being to a course or a person.

There are two basic areas that one ought to pay attention to when devotion is talked about.

The first is God; Man is a spirit. Nothing about man is really physical. The physical is merely a replay of what has been in the spirit. There's this thing about man that requires the God factor; there's this thing in man that re-quires the spiritual. There's a void in man that only God can fill. That's why men get into occultism; into necromancy, mysticism and other stuff in a bid to satisfy that innate longing of his—to fill that void. The more he tries however, to fill that void with what's not God, the more the void is there.

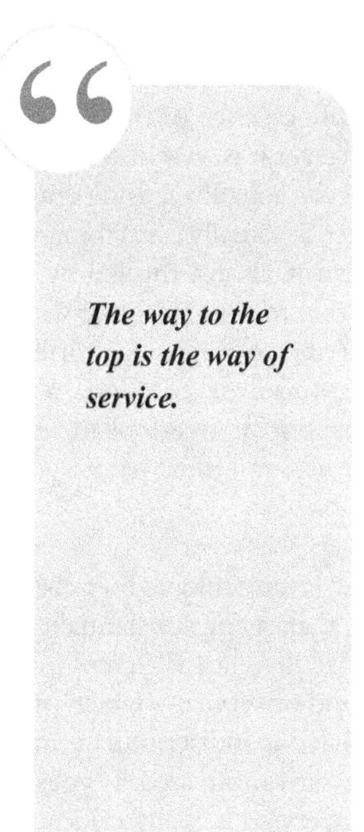

You cannot build anything sustainable without involving the spiritual. You can't build anything remarkable without involving the spiritual. This is why devotion to God has to come first; total commitment to the spirit of God. A lot of people have so many things that they worship. As a believer, I pay keen attention to everything that has to do with my faith because everything I need, comes from there. You need to pay attention to your devotion to God because that's where all your needs will be sorted out from. The bible says that "in him all things consist (Colossians 1:17). This is to say that everything we need is in him, everything we want, everything we need to build with, every idea, every inspiration we need is in him. Every good and perfect gift comes from above, from the father of lights; in whom there's no variableness or shadow of turning. (James 1:17). The light here talks about information but beyond information, it talks about revelation. From this scripture we also understand that gifts come from light; so the more light you have, the more gifts you have; the more gifts you have, the more of a gift you are to your generation. However you can't have more light till you have more of him. The more we commit and devote ourselves to him, the more light we have for ourselves and our generation. How do I mean? It is written that "in him was life and this life became the light of men"; so the more koinonia (fellowship), the more encounter, the more communion, the more devotion we have with this life, the more lit (informed) we get. We become light bearers. Our devotion makes us light bearers. That's why we need to pay keen attention to our devotion. I realized that the things of life try to disconnect us from that which is the essence of our living—the very source of our significance. What-ever it is that distracts you from God and from your spiritual essence is actually causing you so much harm. Because your spiritual essence is actually everything you need to make a mark in your world. Man is always thrilled by the things that are beyond man; so anything that tries to steal that which is beyond man in your life is actually trying to steal your thrilling factor from you. We have to devote ourselves to God. Your relationship with God is a factor that cannot be overlooked. As a person trying to build a sustainable structure, you must have a good relationship with God.

Secondly, if you are going to build any lasting thing, you must be devoted to service. True service is what makes for substantiality in our communities today. I said true because there are different kinds of services. We have the self-righteous kind of service—which picks and decides who to serve. But true ser-vice is indiscriminate in its delivery of service. True service is not reward-motivated. It goes on to serve irrespective of who's involved. Service is really critical; to serve is to meet a need. If what you're building will last then there has to be devotion to service. There are principles that make for true devotion to service. Such principles as;

1. Seek none else's approval except that of purpose. We always go seeking the approval of everybody before going on to do what we need to do. This mistake is why you see someone with an idea being snappy with sharing it because he seeks to get their approval. If you want everybody to be happy

> with you about what you're building, then you will never build anything substantial. To build anything that will stand the test of time, you must pay attention to 'devotion to service' and be sure, that not everybody will be happy with you or with what you're building. I stumbled upon a write up that said "I cannot give you the formula for success but I sure can give you the formula for failure". I probed further to find that the formula for failure is "trying to make everybody happy".

The truth about approval is that you only need the approval of one person; and that person is the one that gave you the gift, the originator of the idea—God. Your attention should mostly be pointed towards what God is saying. If what you're hearing meets his purpose for your life, go ahead and serve your generation. Once God is pleased with what you're doing; once what you're doing is in sync with your purpose, get devoted to service. Whether people approve you of it or not.

As you serve, do not live for applause. It is not wrong for people to commend you for what you're doing but don't get carried away—don't live for applause. Pay full attention to service. De-vote yourself to serve with your whole heart; let neither criticism nor praise get a place in your heart. Pay attention to ser-vice because in life, the days will come when no one will cheer you for what you're doing, when no one will encourage you to keep serving. When those days come, will you stop serving be-cause no one is cheering anymore? You can't build on people's applauses, you can't live on that. Real service is when you do the things that no one takes note of most times; the insignificant and very little things that no one pays attention to. You go ahead and get the job done. Stay devoted to it even when no one is looking. You stick to it; I call it the stick-to-i-iveness of life, the stick-ability, you stay consistently devoted to it. One of the proofs of true service is consistency. You are consistent to your service whether or not there's someone to take note. Whether people applaud you or not; as long as it's producing results in the direction of your purpose, keep delivering! Keep serving.

Devotion is essential to the building and development of anything of value in life. In the place of devotion to God, you find out that you enjoy access to more ideas and inspiration. Isaiah 60:1 tells us to a rise and shine, not because people are around but because light has come; and the glory of the Lord is risen upon you. It now went on to say that "for, behold, the darkness shall cover the earth, and gross darkness the people: but the Lord shall arise upon thee, and his glory shall be seen upon thee. And the Gentiles shall come to thy light, and kings to the brightness of thy rising." Now the problem with most people is that they want gentiles to come before they shine; they want kings to come before they rise. The bible tells us to go ahead and shine; go ahead and serve; go ahead in your devotion to God then gentiles will come to the light and kings to the brightness of your rising.

While you build my friend, keep your devotion to God—our supreme authority intact. While you build, be devoted to service. Prominence belongs to true servants. The mother of Apostles James and John came to Jesus, requesting for her sons' promotion to his left and right hand. Jesus replied and asked her if her children were able to drink of the cup that he was to drink (Matthew 20:20-23). Now that cup was the cup of service. At one other time, the disciples were arguing amongst themselves about who the greatest was; Jesus then informed them that the greatest was the one who made himself servant to others. The way to the top is the way of service.

Stay devoted to God and to service and you will be able to build to completion, things that will shock your world.

www.ingramcontent.com/pod-product-compliance
Lightning Source LLC
LaVergne TN
LVHW050555160826
845677LV00011B/2328

9789789952083